MW01491041

The 15-Minute Anti-Inflammatory Slow Cooker Cookbook

A Collection of Quick, Healthy and 5 Ingredients Recipes That Fight Inflammation and Help You Feel 10 Years Younger Without Sacrificing Taste

Paxton Chisholm

© Copyright 2025 by Paxton Chisholm - All rights reserved.

The purpose of this text is to present accurate and trustworthy information on the facts and topic covered. from a policy statement that was equally accepted and authorized by an American Bar Association committee and a committee of associations and publishers.

This text may not be reproduced, duplicated, or distributed in any way, whether in print or electronic format. All rights protected.

Since all of the material presented here is accurate and consistent, the recipient and reader bear full responsibility for any liability resulting from the use or abuse of any procedures, guidelines, or directions in this document, whether due to negligence or other causes. In no event will the publication be held accountable for any recovery, damages, or monetary loss that can be directly or indirectly linked to the material presented here.

Each author is the owner of any copyrights not owned by the publisher.

Since the material presented here is intended solely for informative purposes, it can be applied broadly. The information is provided without any type of contract or guarantee.

Unauthorized use of trademarks occurs, when trademarks are published without the owner's consent or approval. The brands and trademarks in this book are all owned by their respective owners and are solely used for illustration purposes; they are not associated with this book.

Table of Content

CHAPTER 4: DUMP-AND-GO DINNERS FOR EFFORTLESS HEALING 35

CHAPTER 5: GUT-HEALING SIDES, GRAINS & VEGETABLES 45

CHAPTER 6: HEALING DRINKS & ELIXIRS FOR ALL-DAY ENERGY 53

SCAN THE QR CODE TO ACCESS THE BONUS

Chapter 1: Anti-Inflammatory Cooking Made Simple

Cooking healthy meals shouldn't feel like an uphill battle. The slow cooker is the ultimate tool for making anti-inflammatory eating effortless, turning simple ingredients into nourishing meals with minimal effort. By mastering a few key techniques—quick prep, smart pantry stocking, essential healing ingredients, allergy-friendly swaps, and batch cooking—you remove the guesswork and make clean, healing meals part of your daily routine without stress or extra time in the kitchen.

The 10-Minute Prep Method: Save Time and Still Eat Healthy

Time is the number one excuse people use for not eating healthier. "I don't have time to cook" is the silent killer of good intentions, the reason takeout wins over home-cooked meals. But here's the thing—eating well doesn't have to be time-consuming. You don't need to spend hours chopping, stirring, or hovering over a stove. The **10-Minute Prep Method** is the key to making anti-inflammatory meals work for your busy life.

The idea is simple: **you spend no more than 10 minutes preparing your ingredients, and then your slow cooker does the rest.** No complicated steps, no tedious prep work, no mountain of dishes. The goal is efficiency without sacrificing nutrition or flavor.

So how do you do it? The trick is in the way you handle ingredients. Start by **choosing whole foods that require minimal prep.** Think baby spinach instead of whole heads of kale, cherry tomatoes instead of large tomatoes that need slicing, pre-cut butternut squash, or frozen cauliflower florets that go straight from the bag to the slow cooker. These are not shortcuts that compromise nutrition— they're **hacks that eliminate unnecessary work.**

Then, **streamline your chopping process.** When you do need to cut something, make it quick. A rough chop is usually good enough. Onions? Just halve and slice—no need for a perfect dice. Carrots? Give them a rough chop and toss them in. Peppers? Slice them into strips and move on. This isn't a restaurant kitchen; it's your home, and **imperfection is welcome here.**

Another game-changer? **Batch your prep.** If you're chopping garlic for one recipe, chop enough for three. If you're dicing onions, do it once and store portions in airtight containers for the next few meals. This small shift saves **minutes every day that add up fast.**

Spices and seasonings are the soul of anti-inflammatory cooking, but measuring them out every time you cook can slow you down. **Pre-mix your go-to blends** so you're not hunting for turmeric, cumin, and cinnamon every single time. A simple glass jar filled with your favorite spice combo can turn a basic meal into something vibrant in **seconds, not minutes.**

Liquids are another area where people waste time. Pouring, measuring, and mixing sauces or broths individually is inefficient. Instead, **pre-mix common liquid bases** like coconut milk and turmeric, bone broth with miso, or tomato paste with warming spices. When it's time to cook, you simply grab, pour, and go.

One of the biggest mistakes people make is thinking they need to brown meat before slow cooking. Unless you're after a very specific texture, **skip it.** Slow cooking breaks down fibers and melds flavors over time, so that extra step isn't always necessary. If a recipe calls for searing but you're tight on time, move past it—your dish will still be delicious.

The beauty of the **10-Minute Prep Method** is that it **trains you to focus on what actually matters—** getting whole, anti-inflammatory ingredients into your meals **without the time drain.** And once you embrace the simplicity, you'll never go back to complicated meal prep again.

The Essential Slow Cooker Pantry: Must-Have Staples for Anti-Inflammatory Cooking

A well-stocked pantry is what separates stress-free, consistent anti-inflammatory cooking from last-minute scrambles and uninspired meals. The slow cooker thrives on **depth of flavor and nutrient-dense ingredients**, but its magic depends on what you put inside. Without the right pantry staples, you risk bland, forgettable dishes that don't deliver the powerful health benefits you're after.

At the heart of an anti-inflammatory pantry are **foundational ingredients**—versatile, long-lasting, and packed with properties that fight inflammation at the cellular level. These staples ensure that no matter what fresh ingredients you have on hand, you can always build a meal that supports healing.

Spices are the backbone of anti-inflammatory cooking. **Turmeric, ginger, and cinnamon** are non-negotiable. Turmeric's curcumin content is a **direct inflammation-fighter**, but it needs black pepper to unlock its full potential. Ginger adds heat and digestive support, while cinnamon stabilizes blood sugar and enhances natural sweetness without added sugars. Other essentials include **cumin, coriander, smoked paprika, and cayenne**, all of which add dimension and amplify the body's natural healing mechanisms.

Healthy fats are critical, not just for flavor but for absorption of fat-soluble nutrients. **Cold-pressed olive oil, coconut milk, and ghee** provide richness and stability under long cooking times. Olive oil is a powerhouse of **polyphenols and omega-9s**, coconut milk delivers **medium-chain triglycerides (MCTs)** that fuel the brain and reduce inflammation, and ghee—a clarified butter tolerated by many with dairy sensitivities—offers **butyrate, a fatty acid that supports gut health.**

Broths and liquid bases shape the structure of a dish, carrying flavor and infusing every ingredient with depth. **Bone broth is king here**, packed with collagen, amino acids, and minerals that repair the gut lining and ease joint pain. Vegetable broth, miso paste, and coconut aminos provide essential umami for plant-based meals. **Coconut aminos in particular act as a soy sauce alternative without the inflammatory compounds found in most commercial soy products.**

Shelf-stable proteins keep meals balanced and satisfying, even when fresh ingredients run low. **Lentils, quinoa, and canned wild salmon** ensure that you always have a high-protein option ready to go. Lentils cook effortlessly in a slow cooker, absorbing spices and delivering **fiber, iron, and plant-based protein**. Quinoa, one of the only complete plant proteins, offers a neutral base for countless meals. Wild salmon, packed with **omega-3 fatty acids**, supports brain health and combats systemic inflammation.

No anti-inflammatory pantry is complete without **a selection of nutrient-dense add-ins** that boost the healing power of every meal. Chia seeds, ground flaxseeds, and hemp seeds provide **omega-3s, fiber, and protein** while thickening soups and stews naturally. Nuts and seeds—especially walnuts, almonds, and pumpkin seeds—add crunch and essential minerals. And then there's apple cider vinegar, a small but mighty ingredient that enhances digestion, balances blood sugar, and rounds out flavors with a touch of acidity.

Building this pantry is more than just stocking up on ingredients. It's **setting yourself up for success**, ensuring that every meal delivers not only deep, rich flavors but also the anti-inflammatory benefits that help you feel better, move better, and thrive.

The Magic 5: The Top 5 Anti-Inflammatory Ingredients to Use in Every Meal

Not all ingredients are created equal when it comes to fighting inflammation. Some foods work like fuel for the fire—triggering an immune response that leaves the body inflamed, sluggish, and prone to chronic issues. Others act like firefighters, cooling inflammation at its source and supporting cellular repair. If there were a shortcut to anti-inflammatory cooking, it would be knowing which ingredients to rely on **every single day**—the non-negotiables that transform an ordinary meal into something deeply nourishing.

Turmeric is the foundation of an anti-inflammatory diet. Packed with **curcumin, a potent compound that neutralizes inflammation at the molecular level**, turmeric has been studied for its effects on everything from joint pain to brain function. But curcumin doesn't work alone—it needs black pepper to increase its bioavailability. Without it, the body struggles to absorb its benefits. In a slow cooker, turmeric infuses deeply into liquids, creating **rich, golden broths and stews** that work as natural medicine.

Garlic isn't just for flavor—it's one of the most powerful natural anti-inflammatory agents available. When garlic is chopped or crushed, it releases **allicin, a sulfur compound that acts as a natural immune booster,** protecting the body from oxidative stress. The beauty of slow cooking is that garlic's sharp bite mellows into a smooth, savory depth, making it easy to incorporate into nearly every dish. For maximum potency, fresh garlic is always the best choice—pre-minced versions often lose their medicinal qualities.

Ginger does more than just add warmth to a dish—it actively reduces inflammation in the gut, muscles, and joints. Its unique bioactive compounds, **gingerols and shogaols,** work to lower inflammatory markers in the bloodstream, making it especially effective for those dealing with digestive issues or chronic pain. In slow-cooked meals, ginger's spicy brightness softens, lending a subtle heat that pairs well with both sweet and savory flavors. Fresh ginger delivers the highest concentration of benefits, but ground ginger works in a pinch.

Leafy greens—especially **spinach, kale, and Swiss chard**—are like a nutritional insurance policy. They're loaded with **antioxidants, fiber, and chlorophyll**, which help detoxify the body and calm inflammation at a cellular level. Their high vitamin K content supports cardiovascular health and keeps inflammatory responses in check. While some greens can lose texture in long cooking times, adding them toward the end of the process ensures they retain both their nutrients and their vibrant color.

Berries might seem like an unusual staple for slow cooking, but their **anthocyanins—powerful plant compounds responsible for their deep hues—are directly linked to reducing inflammation in the body.** Blueberries, raspberries, and blackberries are particularly high in these compounds, making them an excellent addition to both sweet and savory dishes. In a slow cooker, berries break down beautifully, creating **natural sauces, compotes, and flavor-enhancing reductions** that require no refined sugar.

These five ingredients aren't trendy superfoods—they're time-tested, research-backed essentials that belong in **every anti-inflammatory meal.** Their ability to support the body's healing processes is unmatched, and when used consistently, they lay the groundwork for lasting wellness.

Easy Substitutions for Common Allergies (Gluten-Free, Dairy-Free, Nut-Free)

Cooking should never feel like an obstacle course, but for those dealing with food allergies or sensitivities, that's exactly what it can become. One wrong ingredient can trigger inflammation, digestive distress, or even more serious reactions. The good news is that most traditional ingredients have anti-inflammatory substitutes that don't just **work**—they often taste better, offer more nutrients, and elevate the dish in unexpected ways.

Gluten lurks in more than just bread and pasta. It hides in sauces, spice blends, broths, and even some unexpected processed foods labeled as "healthy." But eliminating gluten doesn't mean eliminating flavor. Swapping out traditional wheat-based ingredients for naturally gluten-free options is simple when you know what to look for. Instead of regular flour, almond flour or coconut flour offers a **protein-rich, fiber-filled alternative** that creates a slightly nutty depth in slow-cooked dishes. For thickening soups and stews, arrowroot powder or tapioca starch performs just as well as flour without any of the inflammatory effects. If a recipe calls for soy sauce, which contains wheat, coconut aminos provide the same umami punch without the gluten overload.

Dairy is one of the most common inflammatory triggers, yet many people struggle to replace it because of its **richness and texture** in recipes. The solution isn't just about removing dairy—it's about replacing it with ingredients that bring creaminess without the consequences. Full-fat coconut milk is the easiest alternative for slow-cooked meals, offering the same luxurious mouthfeel as heavy cream without disrupting digestion. If a dish needs cheese-like depth, nutritional yeast adds a **savory, umami quality** that mimics Parmesan. Butter can be replaced with ghee, which is clarified to remove lactose and casein, making it far easier to digest while still offering the familiar, golden richness. Those avoiding all dairy completely can turn to avocado oil or olive oil for similar fat content and cooking stability.

Nuts might be nutrient-dense, but they can also be a major allergen. Many plant-based or dairy-free recipes rely on cashews for creaminess, almond flour for structure, and peanut butter for flavor, leaving those with nut allergies feeling excluded from healthier food choices. Fortunately, there are **plenty of alternatives** that achieve the same results. Sunflower seed butter can replace peanut butter in sauces and spreads, offering the same creamy texture and healthy fat profile. For baking or thickening, ground flaxseeds or coconut flour work in place of almond flour, keeping the integrity of the dish intact. Tahini, made from sesame seeds, brings a nutty depth to slow-cooked stews and sauces without triggering nut allergies.

Making substitutions isn't about sacrificing taste or texture—it's about **understanding how ingredients function** so you can swap them effortlessly. Once you know which replacements work best, adapting recipes to be allergen-friendly becomes second nature. Instead of seeing food restrictions as limitations, they become opportunities to **create meals that heal, nourish, and support the body without compromise.**

Batch Cooking & Meal Prepping Hacks to Save Time and Money

Cooking from scratch every day isn't realistic. Life moves fast, and between work, family, and the endless to-do lists, most people don't have time to start fresh in the kitchen every night. That's why batch cooking and meal prepping aren't just time-savers—they're the key to sticking with an anti-inflammatory lifestyle without stress or burnout. The slow cooker is the perfect tool for this approach, turning bulk ingredients into ready-to-go meals that **reduce decision fatigue, eliminate last-minute scrambling, and make it easy to nourish your body even on your busiest days.**

The foundation of batch cooking is **cooking once, eating multiple times.** Instead of making one meal at a time, you prepare ingredients or full dishes in large enough quantities to last for several meals. A slow cooker excels at this because it allows for **passive cooking**—you throw everything in, walk away, and come back hours later to a meal that's ready to be portioned and stored. The key is choosing recipes that hold up well in the fridge or freezer, so they retain their texture and flavor over time.

Some ingredients work better than others for batch cooking. **Legumes, grains, and roasted vegetables** are ideal for prepping in bulk because they maintain their structure even after reheating. Chickpeas and lentils can be cooked in large batches and repurposed for soups, salads, or grain bowls. Brown rice and quinoa hold their integrity and absorb flavors beautifully when stored in broths or sauces. Roasted root vegetables, like sweet potatoes and carrots, keep their texture well and add instant nourishment to any dish.

One of the most effective meal prepping strategies is **building mix-and-match components** rather than full meals. Instead of making a single dish that gets repeated throughout the week, cook individual ingredients that can be assembled in different ways. If you slow-cook a batch of shredded turmeric chicken, it can be used in tacos one night, tossed into a salad the next, and mixed into a warming soup later in the week. Prepped grains, roasted vegetables, and a homemade anti-inflammatory dressing can be combined in endless variations, ensuring that meals stay fresh and exciting.

Portioning correctly is just as important as cooking in bulk. If food isn't stored in a way that makes it easy to grab and use, it's likely to be forgotten and wasted. Dividing meals into **single-serving glass containers** makes reheating effortless and keeps food fresher for longer. Freezing meals in **individual portions** ensures you always have a quick, healthy option ready to go. Silicone freezer trays work well for storing soups and stews in small, pop-out portions that can be thawed as needed.

Batch cooking and meal prepping aren't just about efficiency—they remove the stress of deciding what to eat, making it effortless to stick to an anti-inflammatory diet. By taking advantage of the slow cooker's ability to transform ingredients into **nutrient-dense, ready-to-eat meals,** you create a system where healthy eating is no longer a struggle. It becomes automatic.

Chapter 2: Energizing Breakfasts to Start Your Day Right

GOLDEN TURMERIC OATMEAL WITH CHIA & ALMONDS

P.T.: 5 minutes (preparation), 6 hours (cooking)

Ingr.:

- ½ cup steel-cut oats
- 1 ½ cups almond milk
- ½ tsp turmeric powder
- 1 tbsp chia seeds
- 1 tbsp sliced almonds

Serv.: 2

Cooking Method: Slow Cooker

Procedure:

Combine oats, almond milk, turmeric, and chia seeds in the slow cooker, stirring to blend. Cover and cook on low for 6 hours until thick and creamy. Stir well before serving, then top with sliced almonds for added crunch. Serve warm.

N.V.: Cal. 220 | Fat 9g | Carb. 31g | Prot. 6g

CINNAMON-SPICED APPLE QUINOA PORRIDGE

P.T.: 5 minutes (preparation), 4 hours (cooking)

Ingr.:

- ½ cup quinoa, rinsed
- 1 cup coconut milk
- 1 small apple, diced
- ½ tsp cinnamon
- 1 tbsp maple syrup

Serv.: 2

Cooking Method: Slow Cooker

Procedure:

Add quinoa, coconut milk, apple, and cinnamon to the slow cooker, stirring to combine. Cook on low for 4 hours until the quinoa is tender. Stir in maple syrup, adjust sweetness if needed, and serve warm.

N.V.: Cal. 230 | Fat 7g | Carb. 36g | Prot. 6g

BERRY BLISS OVERNIGHT SLOW COOKER CHIA PUDDING

P.T.: 5 minutes (preparation), 8 hours (cooking)

Ingr.:

- ¼ cup chia seeds
- 1 ½ cups almond milk
- ½ cup mixed berries
- 1 tbsp honey
- ½ tsp vanilla extract

Serv.: 2

Cooking Method: Slow Cooker

Procedure:

Mix chia seeds, almond milk, honey, and vanilla in the slow cooker, stirring well. Cover and cook on low for 8 hours, stirring once halfway. Fold in mixed berries before serving. Chill or enjoy warm.

N.V.: Cal. 200 | Fat 9g | Carb. 28g | Prot. 5g

SLOW COOKER MATCHA COCONUT RICE PUDDING

P.T.: 5 minutes (preparation), 3 hours (cooking)

Ingr.:

- ½ cup jasmine rice
- 1 ½ cups coconut milk
- ½ tsp matcha powder
- 1 tbsp honey
- ½ tsp vanilla extract

Serv.: 2

Cooking Method: Slow Cooker

Procedure:

Combine rice, coconut milk, and matcha powder in the slow cooker, stirring well. Cook on low for 3 hours, stirring occasionally. Once creamy, mix in honey and vanilla before serving. Enjoy warm or chilled.

N.V.: Cal. 250 | Fat 12g | Carb. 35g | Prot. 4g

WARM BANANA WALNUT BREAKFAST BAKE

P.T.: 5 minutes (preparation), 4 hours (cooking)

Ingr.:

- 1 ripe banana, mashed
- ½ cup rolled oats
- 1 cup almond milk
- 1 tbsp chopped walnuts
- ½ tsp cinnamon

Serv.: 2

Cooking Method: Slow Cooker

Procedure:

Mash banana in the slow cooker, then stir in oats, almond milk, and cinnamon. Cook on low for 4 hours, stirring once. Sprinkle with walnuts before serving. Serve warm for a naturally sweet start.

N.V.: Cal. 230 | Fat 8g | Carb. 36g | Prot. 6g

ANTI-INFLAMMATORY SWEET POTATO & GINGER BREAKFAST MASH

P.T.: 5 minutes (preparation), 5 hours (cooking)

Ingr.:

- 1 medium sweet potato, cubed
- 1 cup almond milk
- ½ tsp ground ginger
- 1 tbsp maple syrup
- 1 tbsp crushed pecans

Serv.: 2

Cooking Method: Slow Cooker

Procedure:

Add sweet potato, almond milk, and ginger to the slow cooker, stirring to coat. Cook on low for 5 hours until tender. Mash with a fork, mix in maple syrup, and top with pecans before serving.

N.V.: Cal. 220 | Fat 7g | Carb. 35g | Prot. 4g

SLOW COOKER ALMOND BUTTER & FLAXSEED BREAKFAST BARS

P.T.: 5 minutes (preparation), 3 hours (cooking)

Ingr.:

- ½ cup rolled oats
- 2 tbsp almond butter
- 1 tbsp ground flaxseeds
- 1 tbsp honey
- 1 tsp cinnamon

Serv.: 2

Cooking Method: Slow Cooker

Procedure:

Mix oats, almond butter, flaxseeds, honey, and cinnamon in the slow cooker. Press into an even layer and cook on low for 3 hours. Let cool before slicing into bars. Best served at room temperature.

N.V.: Cal. 210 | Fat 9g | Carb. 30g | Prot. 5g

TURMERIC-SPICED CARROT CAKE OATMEAL

P.T.: 5 minutes (preparation), 6 hours (cooking)

Ingr.:

- ½ cup steel-cut oats
- 1 cup coconut milk
- ½ cup grated carrot
- ½ tsp turmeric
- 1 tbsp raisins

Serv.: 2

Cooking Method: Slow Cooker

Procedure:

Combine oats, coconut milk, carrot, turmeric, and raisins in the slow cooker. Cook on low for 6 hours, stirring once halfway. Serve warm with extra coconut milk if desired.

N.V.: Cal. 240 | Fat 10g | Carb. 34g | Prot. 5g

COCONUT GOLDEN MILK BREAKFAST FARRO

P.T.: 5 minutes (preparation), 5 hours (cooking)

Ingr.:

- ½ cup farro
- 1 ½ cups coconut milk
- ½ tsp turmeric
- ½ tsp cinnamon
- 1 tbsp maple syrup

Serv.: 2

Cooking Method: Slow Cooker

Procedure:

Add farro, coconut milk, turmeric, and cinnamon to the slow cooker, stirring well. Cook on low for 5 hours until tender. Stir in maple syrup before serving for a warm, creamy breakfast.

N.V.: Cal. 260 | Fat 11g | Carb. 37g | Prot. 7g

SLOW COOKER BLUEBERRY BASIL CHIA PUDDING

P.T.: 5 minutes (preparation), 8 hours (cooking)

Ingr.:

- ¼ cup chia seeds
- 1 ½ cups almond milk
- ½ cup blueberries
- ½ tsp vanilla extract
- 1 tsp honey

Serv.: 2

Cooking Method: Slow Cooker

Procedure:

Whisk together chia seeds, almond milk, vanilla, and honey in the slow cooker. Cover and cook on low for 8 hours. Fold in blueberries before serving. Serve chilled or warm.

N.V.: Cal. 200 | Fat 9g | Carb. 28g | Prot. 5g

PUMPKIN & CINNAMON SPICED OVERNIGHT STEEL-CUT OATS

P.T.: 5 minutes (preparation), 6 hours (cooking)

Ingr.:

- ½ cup steel-cut oats
- 1 ½ cups almond milk
- ¼ cup pumpkin purée
- ½ tsp cinnamon
- 1 tsp maple syrup

Serv.: 2

Cooking Method: Slow Cooker

Procedure:

Combine oats, almond milk, pumpkin purée, and cinnamon in the slow cooker, stirring well. Cover and cook on low for 6 hours until thick. Stir in maple syrup before serving warm.

N.V.: Cal. 220 | Fat 5g | Carb. 36g | Prot. 6g

HEALING APPLE CIDER VINEGAR & HONEY OATMEAL

P.T.: 5 minutes (preparation), 5 hours (cooking)

Ingr.:

- ½ cup rolled oats
- 1 ½ cups water
- 1 small apple, diced
- 1 tsp apple cider vinegar
- 1 tsp honey

Serv.: 2

Cooking Method: Slow Cooker

Procedure:

Place oats, water, and diced apple in the slow cooker, stirring to combine. Cover and cook on low for 5 hours. Stir in apple cider vinegar and honey just before serving warm.

N.V.: Cal. 180 | Fat 3g | Carb. 32g | Prot. 4g

WALNUT & DARK CHERRY SLOW COOKER GRANOLA

P.T.: 5 minutes (preparation), 3 hours (cooking)

Ingr.:

- 1 cup rolled oats
- 2 tbsp chopped walnuts
- ¼ cup dried dark cherries
- 1 tbsp honey
- ½ tsp cinnamon

Serv.: 2

Cooking Method: Slow Cooker

Procedure:

Mix oats, walnuts, and cinnamon in the slow cooker, then drizzle with honey. Cook on low for 3 hours, stirring occasionally. Stir in dried cherries and allow to cool before serving.

N.V.: Cal. 250 | Fat 9g | Carb. 38g | Prot. 5g

SLOW COOKER GINGER-TURMERIC PEAR COMPOTE

P.T.: 5 minutes (preparation), 4 hours (cooking)

Ingr.:

- 2 ripe pears, peeled and diced
- ½ tsp ground turmeric
- ½ tsp grated ginger
- 1 tsp maple syrup
- ¼ cup water

Serv.: 2

Cooking Method: Slow Cooker

Procedure:

Combine pears, turmeric, ginger, maple syrup, and water in the slow cooker, stirring gently. Cover and cook on low for 4 hours until soft. Mash lightly and serve warm.

N.V.: Cal. 160 | Fat 1g | Carb. 38g | Prot. 1g

CACAO & AVOCADO SLOW COOKER PROTEIN PUDDING

P.T.: 5 minutes (preparation), 2 hours (cooking)

Ingr.:

- 1 ripe avocado
- 1 cup almond milk
- 2 tbsp cacao powder
- 1 tbsp honey
- ½ tsp vanilla extract

Serv.: 2

Cooking Method: Slow Cooker

Procedure:

Blend avocado, almond milk, cacao powder, honey, and vanilla until smooth. Transfer to the slow cooker and cook on low for 2 hours, stirring occasionally. Let cool before serving.

N.V.: Cal. 220 | Fat 12g | Carb. 25g | Prot. 4g

SLOW COOKER FLAXSEED & COCONUT MUFFIN BITES

P.T.: 5 minutes (preparation), 3 hours (cooking)

Ingr.:

- ½ cup almond flour
- 1 tbsp ground flaxseeds
- 1 tbsp shredded coconut
- 1 tsp honey
- ½ tsp baking powder

Serv.: 2

Cooking Method: Slow Cooker

Procedure:

Combine all ingredients in a bowl and mix until smooth. Pour batter into silicone muffin molds and place in the slow cooker. Cook on low for 3 hours until firm. Let cool before serving.

N.V.: Cal. 200 | Fat 12g | Carb. 18g | Prot. 5g

SPICED CARDAMOM & ORANGE QUINOA BREAKFAST BOWL

P.T.: 5 minutes (preparation), 4 hours (cooking)

Ingr.:

- ½ cup quinoa, rinsed
- 1 ½ cups coconut milk
- ½ tsp cardamom
- 1 tsp orange zest
- 1 tsp maple syrup

Serv.: 2

Cooking Method: Slow Cooker

Procedure:

Place quinoa, coconut milk, cardamom, and orange zest in the slow cooker, stirring well. Cover and cook on low for 4 hours. Stir in maple syrup before serving warm.

N.V.: Cal. 230 | Fat 9g | Carb. 34g | Prot. 5g

ANTI-INFLAMMATORY GOLDEN RAISIN & GINGER MILLET PORRIDGE

P.T.: 5 minutes (preparation), 5 hours (cooking)

Ingr.:

- ½ cup millet
- 1 ½ cups almond milk
- ¼ cup golden raisins
- ½ tsp ground ginger
- 1 tsp honey

Serv.: 2

Cooking Method: Slow Cooker

Procedure:

Combine millet, almond milk, golden raisins, and ginger in the slow cooker, stirring well. Cover and cook on low for 5 hours until creamy. Stir in honey before serving warm.

N.V.: Cal. 210 | Fat 6g | Carb. 35g | Prot. 5g

SLOW COOKER BERRY & HEMP SEED BREAKFAST CRUMBLE

P.T.: 5 minutes (preparation), 2 hours (cooking)

Ingr.:

- 1 cup mixed berries
- ¼ cup rolled oats
- 1 tbsp hemp seeds
- 1 tsp honey
- ½ tsp cinnamon

Serv.: 2

Cooking Method: Slow Cooker

Procedure:

Toss berries with honey and cinnamon in the slow cooker. Sprinkle oats and hemp seeds over the top. Cover and cook on low for 2 hours until berries are bubbling. Serve warm.

N.V.: Cal. 180 | Fat 6g | Carb. 28g | Prot. 4g

COCONUT & ALMOND BUTTER SLOW COOKER BREAKFAST CAKE

P.T.: 5 minutes (preparation), 3 hours (cooking)

Ingr.:

- ½ cup almond flour
- 1 tbsp almond butter
- 1 tbsp shredded coconut
- 1 tsp honey
- ½ tsp baking powder

Serv.: 2

Cooking Method: Slow Cooker

Procedure:

Mix all ingredients in a bowl until smooth. Pour into a greased slow cooker and cook on low for 3 hours until set. Let cool slightly before serving.

N.V.: Cal. 220 | Fat 14g | Carb. 18g | Prot. 6g

Chapter 3: Comforting Soups & Stews for Deep Healing

GOLDEN TURMERIC & GINGER CARROT SOUP

P.T.: 5 minutes (preparation), 4 hours (cooking)

Ingr.:

- 2 cups diced carrots
- 1 ½ cups vegetable broth
- 1 tsp turmeric
- ½ tsp grated ginger
- 1 tsp coconut oil

Serv.: 2

Cooking Method: Slow Cooker

Procedure:

Add carrots, vegetable broth, turmeric, and ginger to the slow cooker, stirring to combine. Cover and cook on low for 4 hours until the carrots are soft. Blend the mixture until smooth, then stir in coconut oil before serving warm.

N.V.: Cal. 150 | Fat 5g | Carb. 25g | Prot. 2g

SLOW COOKER CURRIED SWEET POTATO & COCONUT SOUP

P.T.: 5 minutes (preparation), 5 hours (cooking)

Ingr.:

- 1 medium sweet potato, cubed
- 1 ½ cups coconut milk
- ½ tsp curry powder
- ½ tsp ground cumin
- ½ cup water

Serv.: 2

Cooking Method: Slow Cooker

Procedure:

Place sweet potatoes, coconut milk, curry powder, cumin, and water into the slow cooker, stirring well. Cover and cook on low for 5 hours until the sweet potatoes are soft. Blend until creamy and serve warm.

N.V.: Cal. 220 | Fat 12g | Carb. 30g | Prot. 3g

HEALING BONE BROTH & MUSHROOM ELIXIR

P.T.: 5 minutes (preparation), 6 hours (cooking)

Ingr.:

- 2 cups bone broth
- ½ cup sliced mushrooms
- ½ tsp grated ginger
- ½ tsp turmeric
- 1 tsp apple cider vinegar

Serv.: 2

Cooking Method: Slow Cooker

Procedure:

Combine all ingredients in the slow cooker and stir gently. Cover and cook on low for 6 hours, allowing flavors to infuse deeply. Strain if desired and serve warm as a nourishing elixir.

N.V.: Cal. 80 | Fat 2g | Carb. 5g | Prot. 9g

ANTI-INFLAMMATORY BUTTERNUT SQUASH & APPLE SOUP

P.T.: 5 minutes (preparation), 5 hours (cooking)

Ingr.:

- 1 cup diced butternut squash
- 1 small apple, chopped
- 1 ½ cups vegetable broth
- ½ tsp cinnamon
- ½ tsp turmeric

Serv.: 2

Cooking Method: Slow Cooker

Procedure:

Add butternut squash, apple, broth, cinnamon, and turmeric to the slow cooker and stir well. Cover and cook on low for 5 hours until the squash is tender. Blend the soup until smooth and serve warm.

N.V.: Cal. 170 | Fat 1g | Carb. 38g | Prot. 2g

DETOXIFYING GREEN SOUP WITH KALE & BROCCOLI

P .T.: 5 minutes (preparation), 4 hours (cooking)

Ingr.:

- 1 cup chopped kale
- 1 cup broccoli florets
- 1 ½ cups vegetable broth
- ½ tsp garlic powder
- 1 tsp lemon juice

Serv.: 2

Cooking Method: Slow Cooker

Procedure:

Place kale, broccoli, broth, and garlic powder in the slow cooker, stirring to mix. Cover and cook on low for 4 hours until vegetables soften. Blend until smooth, then stir in lemon juice before serving.

N.V.: Cal. 120 | Fat 2g | Carb. 22g | Prot. 5g

SLOW COOKER RED LENTIL & TOMATO HEALING STEW

P.T.: 5 minutes (preparation), 5 hours (cooking)

Ingr.:

- ½ cup red lentils
- 1 cup diced tomatoes
- 1 ½ cups vegetable broth
- ½ tsp ground cumin
- ½ tsp turmeric

Serv.: 2

Cooking Method: Slow Cooker

Procedure:

Combine lentils, tomatoes, broth, cumin, and turmeric in the slow cooker, mixing well. Cover and cook on low for 5 hours until lentils break down. Stir well before serving warm.

N.V.: Cal. 210 | Fat 1g | Carb. 38g | Prot. 12g

GINGER-GARLIC CHICKEN SOUP FOR IMMUNITY

P.T.: 5 minutes (preparation), 6 hours (cooking)

Ingr.:

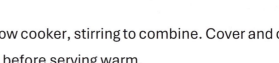

- 1 small chicken breast, cubed
- 1 ½ cups bone broth
- ½ tsp grated ginger
- ½ tsp minced garlic
- ½ cup chopped carrots

Serv.: 2

Cooking Method: Slow Cooker

Procedure:

Add chicken, broth, ginger, garlic, and carrots to the slow cooker, stirring to combine. Cover and cook on low for 6 hours until the chicken is tender. Stir well before serving warm.

N.V.: Cal. 190 | Fat 4g | Carb. 10g | Prot. 28g

ANTI-INFLAMMATORY TURMERIC & CAULIFLOWER SOUP

P.T.: 5 minutes (preparation), 4 hours (cooking)

Ingr.:

- 1 cup cauliflower florets
- 1 ½ cups vegetable broth
- ½ tsp turmeric
- ½ tsp ground black pepper
- 1 tsp olive oil

Serv.: 2

Cooking Method: Slow Cooker

Procedure:

Place cauliflower, broth, turmeric, and black pepper in the slow cooker, stirring gently. Cover and cook on low for 4 hours until cauliflower is soft. Blend until smooth, then stir in olive oil before serving.

N.V.: Cal. 110 | Fat 4g | Carb. 15g | Prot. 3g

GUT-HEALING MISO & SHIITAKE MUSHROOM BROTH

P.T.: 5 minutes (preparation), 5 hours (cooking)

Ingr.:

- 2 cups vegetable broth
- ½ cup sliced shiitake mushrooms
- 1 tbsp miso paste
- ½ tsp grated ginger
- ½ tsp sesame oil

Serv.: 2

Cooking Method: Slow Cooker

Procedure:

Combine broth, mushrooms, ginger, and miso paste in the slow cooker, stirring well. Cover and cook on low for 5 hours until flavors develop. Stir in sesame oil just before serving warm.

N.V.: Cal. 100 | Fat 3g | Carb. 10g | Prot. 5g

SLOW COOKER SPICED PUMPKIN & COCONUT SOUP

P.T.: 5 minutes (preparation), 4 hours (cooking)

Ingr.:

- 1 cup pumpkin purée
- 1 ½ cups coconut milk
- ½ tsp cinnamon
- ½ tsp ground nutmeg
- 1 tsp honey

Serv.: 2

Cooking Method: Slow Cooker

Procedure:

Place pumpkin, coconut milk, cinnamon, and nutmeg into the slow cooker, stirring to combine. Cover and cook on low for 4 hours until flavors meld. Stir in honey before serving warm.

N.V.: Cal. 220 | Fat 12g | Carb. 28g | Prot. 3g

TOMATO, BASIL & CANNELLINI BEAN HEALING STEW

P.T.: 5 minutes (preparation), 5 hours (cooking)

Ingr.:

- 1 cup diced tomatoes
- ½ cup cannellini beans, drained
- 1 ½ cups vegetable broth
- ½ tsp dried basil
- 1 tsp olive oil

Serv.: 2

Cooking Method: Slow Cooker

Procedure:

Combine tomatoes, cannellini beans, broth, and basil in the slow cooker, stirring gently. Cover and cook on low for 5 hours until beans soften. Stir in olive oil before serving warm.

N.V.: Cal. 190 | Fat 5g | Carb. 28g | Prot. 7g

ANTI-INFLAMMATORY GOLDEN BEET & CARROT SOUP

P.T.: 5 minutes (preparation), 4 hours (cooking)

Ingr.:

- 1 cup diced golden beets
- 1 cup diced carrots
- 1 ½ cups vegetable broth
- ½ tsp turmeric
- ½ tsp ground ginger

Serv.: 2

Cooking Method: Slow Cooker

Procedure:

Place beets, carrots, broth, turmeric, and ginger in the slow cooker, stirring well. Cover and cook on low for 4 hours until vegetables are soft. Blend until smooth and serve warm.

N.V.: Cal. 160 | Fat 1g | Carb. 35g | Prot. 3g

CINNAMON-SPICED MOROCCAN CHICKPEA STEW

P.T.: 5 minutes (preparation), 6 hours (cooking)

Ingr.:

- ½ cup canned chickpeas, drained
- 1 cup diced tomatoes
- 1 ½ cups vegetable broth
- ½ tsp cinnamon
- ½ tsp ground cumin

Serv.: 2

Cooking Method: Slow Cooker

Procedure:

Combine chickpeas, tomatoes, broth, cinnamon, and cumin in the slow cooker, stirring to mix. Cover and cook on low for 6 hours until flavors meld. Stir well before serving warm.

N.V.: Cal. 210 | Fat 3g | Carb. 35g | Prot. 8g

LEMON-GINGER DETOX LENTIL SOUP

P.T.: 5 minutes (preparation), 5 hours (cooking)

Ingr.:

- ½ cup red lentils
- 1 ½ cups vegetable broth
- ½ tsp grated ginger
- ½ tsp ground turmeric
- 1 tsp lemon juice

Serv.: 2

Cooking Method: Slow Cooker

Procedure:

Add lentils, broth, ginger, and turmeric to the slow cooker, stirring well. Cover and cook on low for 5 hours until lentils are soft. Stir in lemon juice just before serving.

N.V.: Cal. 180 | Fat 1g | Carb. 32g | Prot. 10g

SLOW COOKER CABBAGE & FENNEL DETOX SOUP

P.T.: 5 minutes (preparation), 4 hours (cooking)

Ingr.:

- 1 cup shredded cabbage
- ½ cup sliced fennel
- 1 ½ cups vegetable broth
- ½ tsp garlic powder
- ½ tsp ground black pepper

Serv.: 2

Cooking Method: Slow Cooker

Procedure:

Combine cabbage, fennel, broth, garlic powder, and black pepper in the slow cooker, stirring well.

Cover and cook on low for 4 hours until vegetables are tender. Stir well before serving warm.

N.V.: Cal. 130 | Fat 1g | Carb. 26g | Prot. 3g

ANTI-INFLAMMATORY THAI-INSPIRED COCONUT LEMONGRASS SOUP

P.T.: 5 minutes (preparation), 5 hours (cooking)

Ingr.:

- 1 ½ cups coconut milk
- ½ cup sliced mushrooms
- 1 tsp lemongrass paste
- ½ tsp grated ginger
- ½ tsp turmeric

Serv.: 2

Cooking Method: Slow Cooker

Procedure:

Place coconut milk, mushrooms, lemongrass, ginger, and turmeric in the slow cooker, stirring well.

Cover and cook on low for 5 hours until flavors meld. Stir before serving warm.

N.V.: Cal. 220 | Fat 14g | Carb. 18g | Prot. 3g

SOOTHING CARROT, TURMERIC & APPLE SOUP

P.T.: 5 minutes (preparation), 4 hours (cooking)

Ingr.:

- 1 cup diced carrots
- 1 small apple, chopped
- 1 ½ cups vegetable broth
- ½ tsp turmeric
- ½ tsp cinnamon

Serv.: 2

Cooking Method: Slow Cooker

Procedure:

Add carrots, apple, broth, turmeric, and cinnamon to the slow cooker, stirring gently. Cover and cook on low for 4 hours until vegetables soften. Blend until smooth and serve warm.

N.V.: Cal. 150 | Fat 1g | Carb. 34g | Prot. 2g

SPICED RED PEPPER & ALMOND SOUP

P.T.: 5 minutes (preparation), 3 hours (cooking)

Ingr.:

- 1 cup roasted red bell peppers
- 1 ½ cups vegetable broth
- 1 tbsp almond butter
- ½ tsp smoked paprika
- ½ tsp ground cumin

Serv.: 2

Cooking Method: Slow Cooker

Procedure:

Blend peppers, broth, almond butter, paprika, and cumin until smooth, then transfer to the slow cooker. Cover and cook on low for 3 hours until flavors develop. Stir before serving warm.

N.V.: Cal. 180 | Fat 8g | Carb. 22g | Prot. 5g

SLOW COOKER ZUCCHINI & LEEK HEALING SOUP

P.T.: 5 minutes (preparation), 4 hours (cooking)

Ingr.:

- 1 cup sliced zucchini
- ½ cup sliced leeks
- 1 ½ cups vegetable broth
- ½ tsp garlic powder
- ½ tsp ground black pepper

Serv.: 2

Cooking Method: Slow Cooker

Procedure:

Combine zucchini, leeks, broth, garlic powder, and black pepper in the slow cooker, stirring gently.

Cover and cook on low for 4 hours until vegetables soften. Blend until smooth and serve warm.

N.V.: Cal. 130 | Fat 2g | Carb. 20g | Prot. 3g

GUT-HEALING COCONUT, GINGER & CAULIFLOWER STEW

P.T.: 5 minutes (preparation), 5 hours (cooking)

Ingr.:

- 1 cup cauliflower florets
- 1 ½ cups coconut milk
- ½ tsp grated ginger
- ½ tsp turmeric
- ½ tsp ground cumin

Serv.: 2

Cooking Method: Slow Cooker

Procedure:

Place cauliflower, coconut milk, ginger, turmeric, and cumin in the slow cooker, stirring well. Cover and cook on low for 5 hours until cauliflower is tender. Stir before serving warm.

N.V.: Cal. 200 | Fat 14g | Carb. 18g | Prot. 4g

Chapter 4: Dump-and-Go Dinners for Effortless Healing

SLOW COOKER LEMON-GARLIC CHICKEN WITH TURMERIC & ROSEMARY

P.T.: 5 minutes (preparation), 6 hours (cooking)

Ingr.:

- 2 small chicken breasts
- 1 cup bone broth
- 1 tsp turmeric
- ½ tsp minced garlic
- ½ tsp dried rosemary

Serv.: 2

Cooking Method: Slow Cooker

Procedure:

Place chicken in the slow cooker and pour the broth over it. Sprinkle turmeric, garlic, and rosemary evenly. Cover and cook on low for 6 hours until the chicken is tender. Shred lightly and mix with the juices before serving.

N.V.: Cal. 210 | Fat 5g | Carb. 2g | Prot. 38g

ANTI-INFLAMMATORY GINGER-TURMERIC SALMON WITH COCONUT BROTH

P.T.: 5 minutes (preparation), 3 hours (cooking)

Ingr.:

- 2 salmon fillets
- 1 cup coconut milk
- ½ tsp turmeric
- ½ tsp grated ginger
- ½ tsp sea salt

Serv.: 2

Cooking Method: Slow Cooker

Procedure:

Place salmon fillets in the slow cooker and pour in the coconut milk. Sprinkle turmeric, ginger, and salt evenly. Cover and cook on low for 3 hours until the salmon is flaky. Serve with the infused broth for extra flavor.

N.V.: Cal. 290 | Fat 20g | Carb. 3g | Prot. 24g

SLOW COOKER MOROCCAN-SPICED CHICKPEAS & SWEET POTATOES

P.T.: 5 minutes (preparation), 5 hours (cooking)

Ingr.:

- ½ cup canned chickpeas, drained
- 1 small sweet potato, cubed
- 1 ½ cups vegetable broth
- ½ tsp cinnamon
- ½ tsp ground cumin

Serv.: 2

Cooking Method: Slow Cooker

Procedure:

Combine chickpeas, sweet potatoes, broth, cinnamon, and cumin in the slow cooker. Stir gently to distribute spices evenly. Cover and cook on low for 5 hours until sweet potatoes are soft. Stir before serving warm.

N.V.: Cal. 240 | Fat 3g | Carb. 42g | Prot. 9g

GOLDEN CAULIFLOWER & LENTIL CURRY WITH COCONUT MILK

P.T.: 5 minutes (preparation), 4 hours (cooking)

Ingr.:

- 1 cup cauliflower florets
- ½ cup red lentils
- 1 ½ cups coconut milk
- ½ tsp turmeric
- ½ tsp ground coriander

Serv.: 2

Cooking Method: Slow Cooker

Procedure:

Place cauliflower, lentils, coconut milk, turmeric, and coriander in the slow cooker, stirring gently. Cover and cook on low for 4 hours until the lentils soften. Stir well and serve warm.

N.V.: Cal. 260 | Fat 12g | Carb. 32g | Prot. 10g

SLOW COOKER GARLIC & HERB QUINOA-STUFFED PEPPERS

P.T.: 5 minutes (preparation), 4 hours (cooking)

Ingr.:

- 2 bell peppers, halved
- ½ cup cooked quinoa
- ½ tsp garlic powder
- ½ tsp dried oregano
- 1 cup vegetable broth

Serv.: 2

Cooking Method: Slow Cooker

Procedure:

Stuff each pepper half with quinoa, garlic powder, and oregano. Arrange them in the slow cooker and pour broth around them. Cover and cook on low for 4 hours until the peppers are soft.

N.V.: Cal. 190 | Fat 2g | Carb. 34g | Prot. 6g

HEALING TURMERIC & GINGER BEEF STEW

P.T.: 5 minutes (preparation), 6 hours (cooking)

Ingr.:

- ½ lb beef stew meat
- 1 ½ cups bone broth
- ½ tsp turmeric
- ½ tsp grated ginger
- ½ cup chopped carrots

Serv.: 2

Cooking Method: Slow Cooker

Procedure:

Place beef, broth, turmeric, ginger, and carrots in the slow cooker. Stir to evenly coat the beef with the spices. Cover and cook on low for 6 hours until beef is tender. Stir before serving.

N.V.: Cal. 320 | Fat 15g | Carb. 12g | Prot. 36g

SLOW COOKER ZESTY LIME & CILANTRO CHICKEN TACOS

P.T.: 5 minutes (preparation), 5 hours (cooking)

Ingr.:

- 2 small chicken breasts
- 1 cup chicken broth
- 1 tsp lime juice
- ½ tsp ground cumin
- 1 tbsp chopped cilantro

Serv.: 2

Cooking Method: Slow Cooker

Procedure:

Place chicken, broth, lime juice, and cumin in the slow cooker and mix well. Cover and cook on low for 5 hours until the chicken is tender. Shred and stir in cilantro before serving.

N.V.: Cal. 220 | Fat 4g | Carb. 3g | Prot. 42g

MISO-GINGER SLOW COOKER TOFU & VEGETABLES

P.T.: 5 minutes (preparation), 4 hours (cooking)

Ingr.:

- ½ block firm tofu, cubed
- 1 cup vegetable broth
- ½ tsp grated ginger
- 1 tsp miso paste
- ½ cup sliced mushrooms

Serv.: 2

Cooking Method: Slow Cooker

Procedure:

Combine tofu, broth, ginger, miso paste, and mushrooms in the slow cooker. Stir to evenly coat the tofu with the broth. Cover and cook on low for 4 hours. Stir gently before serving.

N.V.: Cal. 180 | Fat 7g | Carb. 14g | Prot. 15g

SPICED BUTTERNUT SQUASH & RED LENTIL STEW

P.T.: 5 minutes (preparation), 5 hours (cooking)

Ingr.:

- 1 cup diced butternut squash
- ½ cup red lentils
- 1 ½ cups vegetable broth
- ½ tsp ground cumin
- ½ tsp cinnamon

Serv.: 2

Cooking Method: Slow Cooker

Procedure:

Place butternut squash, lentils, broth, cumin, and cinnamon in the slow cooker and stir well. Cover and cook on low for 5 hours until the lentils soften. Stir before serving warm.

N.V.: Cal. 230 | Fat 2g | Carb. 40g | Prot. 11g

SLOW COOKER COCONUT-LIME SHRIMP WITH ZOODLES

P.T.: 5 minutes (preparation), 3 hours (cooking)

Ingr.:

- ½ lb shrimp, peeled
- 1 cup coconut milk
- 1 tsp lime juice
- ½ tsp ground turmeric
- 1 cup spiralized zucchini

Serv.: 2

Cooking Method: Slow Cooker

Procedure:

Place shrimp, coconut milk, lime juice, and turmeric in the slow cooker, stirring gently. Cover and cook on low for 3 hours until shrimp are cooked through. Serve over fresh zucchini noodles.

N.V.: Cal. 240 | Fat 14g | Carb. 10g | Prot. 28g

CINNAMON-SPICED APPLE & BALSAMIC PORK TENDERLOIN

P.T.: 5 minutes (preparation), 6 hours (cooking)

Ingr.:

- ½ lb pork tenderloin
- 1 small apple, sliced
- 1 tbsp balsamic vinegar
- ½ tsp cinnamon
- ½ cup bone broth

Serv.: 2

Cooking Method: Slow Cooker

Procedure:

Place pork in the slow cooker and top with apple slices. Pour balsamic vinegar and broth over the pork, then sprinkle with cinnamon. Cover and cook on low for 6 hours until tender, then slice and serve.

N.V.: Cal. 270 | Fat 8g | Carb. 12g | Prot. 38g

SLOW COOKER THAI-INSPIRED LEMONGRASS CHICKEN

P.T.: 5 minutes (preparation), 5 hours (cooking)

Ingr.:

- 2 small chicken breasts
- 1 cup coconut milk
- 1 tsp lemongrass paste
- ½ tsp grated ginger
- ½ tsp turmeric

Serv.: 2

Cooking Method: Slow Cooker

Procedure:

Place chicken in the slow cooker and pour coconut milk over it. Add lemongrass, ginger, and turmeric, stirring gently. Cover and cook on low for 5 hours until chicken is tender, then shred before serving.

N.V.: Cal. 290 | Fat 16g | Carb. 4g | Prot. 34g

GINGER-TURMERIC CAULIFLOWER & CHICKPEA TAGINE

P.T.: 5 minutes (preparation), 5 hours (cooking)

Ingr.:

- 1 cup cauliflower florets
- ½ cup canned chickpeas, drained
- 1 ½ cups vegetable broth
- ½ tsp turmeric
- ½ tsp grated ginger

Serv.: 2

Cooking Method: Slow Cooker

Procedure:

Combine cauliflower, chickpeas, broth, turmeric, and ginger in the slow cooker, stirring well. Cover and cook on low for 5 hours until cauliflower is soft. Stir well before serving warm.

N.V.: Cal. 200 | Fat 3g | Carb. 34g | Prot. 9g

ANTI-INFLAMMATORY GARLIC & TURMERIC BALSAMIC BEEF ROAST

P.T.: 5 minutes (preparation), 6 hours (cooking)

Ingr.:

- ½ lb beef roast
- 1 cup bone broth
- 1 tbsp balsamic vinegar
- ½ tsp turmeric
- ½ tsp minced garlic

Serv.: 2

Cooking Method: Slow Cooker

Procedure:

Place beef in the slow cooker and pour broth over it. Add balsamic vinegar, turmeric, and garlic, then stir gently. Cover and cook on low for 6 hours until tender, then slice before serving.

N.V.: Cal. 320 | Fat 14g | Carb. 6g | Prot. 40g

SLOW COOKER COCONUT-CURRY MEATBALLS

P.T.: 5 minutes (preparation), 4 hours (cooking)

Ingr.:

- ½ lb ground turkey
- 1 cup coconut milk
- ½ tsp curry powder
- ½ tsp turmeric
- ½ tsp sea salt

Serv.: 2

Cooking Method: Slow Cooker

Procedure:

Form turkey into small meatballs and place in the slow cooker. Pour in coconut milk, then add curry powder, turmeric, and salt. Cover and cook on low for 4 hours until meatballs are fully cooked.

N.V.: Cal. 280 | Fat 18g | Carb. 5g | Prot. 26g

HEALING LEMON, DILL & GARLIC SALMON FILLETS

P.T.: 5 minutes (preparation), 3 hours (cooking)

Ingr.:

- 2 salmon fillets
- 1 cup bone broth
- 1 tsp lemon juice
- ½ tsp minced garlic
- ½ tsp dried dill

Serv.: 2

Cooking Method: Slow Cooker

Procedure:

Place salmon fillets in the slow cooker and pour broth over them. Add lemon juice, garlic, and dill, then cover and cook on low for 3 hours until the salmon is flaky. Serve with the infused broth.

N.V.: Cal. 270 | Fat 15g | Carb. 2g | Prot. 30g

TURMERIC-SPICED LENTIL & CARROT SOUP WITH CORIANDER

P.T.: 5 minutes (preparation), 5 hours (cooking)

Ingr.:

- ½ cup red lentils
- 1 cup chopped carrots
- 1 ½ cups vegetable broth
- ½ tsp turmeric
- ½ tsp ground coriander

Serv.: 2

Cooking Method: Slow Cooker

Procedure:

Place lentils, carrots, broth, turmeric, and coriander in the slow cooker, stirring well. Cover and cook on low for 5 hours until lentils are soft. Stir before serving warm.

N.V.: Cal. 210 | Fat 1g | Carb. 38g | Prot. 10g

SLOW COOKER HONEY-GARLIC CHICKEN WITH BROCCOLI & CARROTS

P.T.: 5 minutes (preparation), 5 hours (cooking)

Ingr.:

- 2 small chicken breasts
- 1 cup bone broth
- 1 tsp honey
- ½ cup chopped broccoli
- ½ cup chopped carrots

Serv.: 2

Cooking Method: Slow Cooker

Procedure:

Place chicken in the slow cooker and pour in the broth. Stir in honey, then add broccoli and carrots. Cover and cook on low for 5 hours until chicken is tender, then shred before serving.

N.V.: Cal. 240 | Fat 4g | Carb. 12g | Prot. 40g

SLOW COOKER CINNAMON & GINGER-SPICED TURKEY CHILI

P.T.: 5 minutes (preparation), 5 hours (cooking)

Ingr.:

- ½ lb ground turkey
- 1 cup diced tomatoes
- 1 ½ cups vegetable broth
- ½ tsp ground cinnamon
- ½ tsp grated ginger

Serv.: 2

Cooking Method: Slow Cooker

Procedure:

Place turkey, tomatoes, broth, cinnamon, and ginger in the slow cooker, stirring gently. Cover and cook on low for 5 hours, allowing flavors to develop. Stir well before serving warm.

N.V.: Cal. 280 | Fat 8g | Carb. 16g | Prot. 38g

ANTI-INFLAMMATORY BUTTERNUT SQUASH & BLACK BEAN TACOS

P.T.: 5 minutes (preparation), 4 hours (cooking)

Ingr.:

- 1 cup diced butternut squash
- ½ cup canned black beans, drained
- 1 ½ cups vegetable broth
- ½ tsp smoked paprika
- ½ tsp ground cumin

Serv.: 2

Cooking Method: Slow Cooker

Procedure:

Combine squash, black beans, broth, paprika, and cumin in the slow cooker, stirring well. Cover and cook on low for 4 hours until squash is soft. Serve warm in taco shells or lettuce wraps.

N.V.: Cal. 230 | Fat 2g | Carb. 40g | Prot. 10g

Chapter 5: Gut-Healing Sides, Grains & Vegetables

TURMERIC & GINGER-SPICED QUINOA PILAF

P.T.: 5 minutes (preparation), 4 hours (cooking)

Ingr.:

- ½ cup quinoa, rinsed
- 1 ½ cups vegetable broth
- ½ tsp turmeric
- ½ tsp grated ginger
- 1 tsp olive oil

Serv.: 2

Cooking Method: Slow Cooker

Procedure:

Place quinoa, broth, turmeric, and ginger in the slow cooker, stirring to combine. Cover and cook on low for 4 hours until quinoa is tender. Fluff with a fork and drizzle with olive oil before serving.

N.V.: Cal. 220 | Fat 6g | Carb. 36g | Prot. 8g

SLOW COOKER GARLIC & LEMON ROASTED BRUSSELS SPROUTS

P.T.: 5 minutes (preparation), 3 hours (cooking)

Ingr.:

- 1 cup halved Brussels sprouts
- 1 tbsp olive oil
- ½ tsp minced garlic
- ½ tsp lemon zest
- ½ tsp sea salt

Serv.: 2

Cooking Method: Slow Cooker

Procedure:

Toss Brussels sprouts with olive oil, garlic, lemon zest, and salt. Place in the slow cooker and cook on low for 3 hours, stirring occasionally. Serve warm with an extra drizzle of olive oil if desired.

N.V.: Cal. 140 | Fat 8g | Carb. 16g | Prot. 4g

GOLDEN CAULIFLOWER RICE WITH COCONUT & CILANTRO

P.T.: 5 minutes (preparation), 3 hours (cooking)

Ingr.:

- 1 cup riced cauliflower
- 1 cup coconut milk
- ½ tsp turmeric
- ½ tsp ground cumin
- 1 tbsp chopped cilantro

Serv.: 2

Cooking Method: Slow Cooker

Procedure:

Combine cauliflower rice, coconut milk, turmeric, and cumin in the slow cooker, stirring gently.

Cover and cook on low for 3 hours until tender. Stir in cilantro before serving warm.

N.V.: Cal. 180 | Fat 10g | Carb. 14g | Prot. 3g

SLOW COOKER CINNAMON-SPICED CARROTS & APPLES

P.T.: 5 minutes (preparation), 4 hours (cooking)

Ingr.:

- 1 cup sliced carrots
- 1 small apple, diced
- ½ tsp cinnamon
- 1 tsp honey
- ½ cup water

Serv.: 2

Cooking Method: Slow Cooker

Procedure:

Place carrots, apples, cinnamon, honey, and water in the slow cooker, stirring to combine. Cover and cook on low for 4 hours until soft. Stir well before serving warm.

N.V.: Cal. 130 | Fat 1g | Carb. 30g | Prot. 1g

ANTI-INFLAMMATORY SWEET POTATO MASH WITH TURMERIC & COCONUT MILK

P.T.: 5 minutes (preparation), 3 hours (cooking)

Ingr.:

- 1 medium sweet potato, peeled and cubed
- 1 cup coconut milk
- ½ tsp turmeric
- ½ tsp cinnamon
- 1 tsp maple syrup

Serv.: 2

Cooking Method: Slow Cooker

Procedure:

Combine sweet potatoes, coconut milk, turmeric, and cinnamon in the slow cooker. Cover and cook on low for 3 hours until soft. Mash with a fork, stir in maple syrup, and serve warm.

N.V.: Cal. 210 | Fat 7g | Carb. 35g | Prot. 2g

SLOW COOKER MISO-GINGER GLAZED MUSHROOMS

P.T.: 5 minutes (preparation), 3 hours (cooking)

Ingr.:

- 1 cup sliced mushrooms
- 1 tbsp miso paste
- ½ tsp grated ginger
- ½ tsp sesame oil
- ½ cup vegetable broth

Serv.: 2

Cooking Method: Slow Cooker

Procedure:

Combine mushrooms, miso paste, ginger, sesame oil, and broth in the slow cooker, stirring gently. Cover and cook on low for 3 hours until mushrooms are tender. Stir well before serving.

N.V.: Cal. 110 | Fat 4g | Carb. 14g | Prot. 3g

CURRIED LENTILS & SPINACH WITH GARLIC & CUMIN

P.T.: 5 minutes (preparation), 4 hours (cooking)

Ingr.:

- ½ cup red lentils
- 1 cup chopped spinach
- 1 ½ cups vegetable broth
- ½ tsp ground cumin
- ½ tsp minced garlic

Serv.: 2

Cooking Method: Slow Cooker

Procedure:

Place lentils, spinach, broth, cumin, and garlic in the slow cooker, stirring gently. Cover and cook on low for 4 hours until lentils are soft. Stir well before serving warm.

N.V.: Cal. 190 | Fat 2g | Carb. 34g | Prot. 12g

SLOW COOKER SPICED RED CABBAGE & APPLE SLAW

P.T.: 5 minutes (preparation), 4 hours (cooking)

Ingr.:

- 1 cup shredded red cabbage
- 1 small apple, thinly sliced
- ½ tsp cinnamon
- 1 tbsp apple cider vinegar
- ½ tsp sea salt

Serv.: 2

Cooking Method: Slow Cooker

Procedure:

Combine cabbage, apple, cinnamon, apple cider vinegar, and salt in the slow cooker, stirring well. Cover and cook on low for 4 hours until softened. Stir before serving warm.

N.V.: Cal. 110 | Fat 1g | Carb. 28g | Prot. 2g

ANTI-INFLAMMATORY GARLIC & HERB BUTTERNUT SQUASH

P.T.: 5 minutes (preparation), 4 hours (cooking)

Ingr.:

- 1 cup diced butternut squash
- 1 tbsp olive oil
- ½ tsp minced garlic
- ½ tsp dried oregano
- ½ tsp sea salt

Serv.: 2

Cooking Method: Slow Cooker

Procedure:

Place butternut squash, olive oil, garlic, oregano, and salt in the slow cooker, stirring gently. Cover and cook on low for 4 hours until soft. Stir before serving warm.

N.V.: Cal. 160 | Fat 7g | Carb. 26g | Prot. 2g

SLOW COOKER CILANTRO-LIME BROWN RICE WITH AVOCADO

P.T.: 5 minutes (preparation), 5 hours (cooking)

Ingr.:

- ½ cup brown rice
- 1 ½ cups vegetable broth
- 1 tsp lime juice
- 1 tbsp chopped cilantro
- ½ small avocado, sliced

Serv.: 2

Cooking Method: Slow Cooker

Procedure:

Place rice, broth, and lime juice in the slow cooker, stirring gently. Cover and cook on low for 5 hours until rice is tender. Stir in cilantro and top with avocado before serving.

N.V.: Cal. 210 | Fat 6g | Carb. 38g | Prot. 5g

HEALING BONE BROTH & TURMERIC RICE

P.T.: 5 minutes (preparation), 4 hours (cooking)

Ingr.:

- ½ cup jasmine rice
- 1 ½ cups bone broth
- ½ tsp turmeric
- ½ tsp garlic powder
- ½ tsp sea salt

Serv.: 2

Cooking Method: Slow Cooker

Procedure:

Place rice, bone broth, turmeric, garlic powder, and sea salt in the slow cooker, stirring gently. Cover and cook on low for 4 hours until rice is tender. Fluff with a fork before serving warm.

N.V.: Cal. 190 | Fat 2g | Carb. 36g | Prot. 6g

SLOW COOKER ROASTED BEETS WITH ORANGE & GINGER

P.T.: 5 minutes (preparation), 4 hours (cooking)

Ingr.:

- 1 cup diced beets
- ½ tsp grated ginger
- 1 tsp orange zest
- ½ tsp olive oil
- ½ tsp sea salt

Serv.: 2

Cooking Method: Slow Cooker

Procedure:

Toss beets with ginger, orange zest, olive oil, and sea salt. Place in the slow cooker and cover. Cook on low for 4 hours until tender, stirring once halfway through cooking. Serve warm.

N.V.: Cal. 150 | Fat 4g | Carb. 28g | Prot. 3g

WARM ANTI-INFLAMMATORY BROCCOLI & KALE SLAW

P.T.: 5 minutes (preparation), 3 hours (cooking)

Ingr.:

- 1 cup chopped broccoli
- ½ cup shredded kale
- ½ tsp turmeric
- ½ tsp apple cider vinegar
- 1 tsp olive oil

Serv.: 2

Cooking Method: Slow Cooker

Procedure:

Combine broccoli, kale, turmeric, apple cider vinegar, and olive oil in the slow cooker, stirring well.

Cover and cook on low for 3 hours, stirring once. Serve warm as a side or salad base.

N.V.: Cal. 120 | Fat 5g | Carb. 14g | Prot. 4g

SLOW COOKER SPAGHETTI SQUASH WITH GARLIC & BASIL PESTO

P.T.: 5 minutes (preparation), 4 hours (cooking)

Ingr.:

- ½ small spaghetti squash, halved
- 1 tbsp olive oil
- ½ tsp minced garlic
- 1 tbsp basil pesto
- ½ tsp sea salt

Serv.: 2

Cooking Method: Slow Cooker

Procedure:

Place spaghetti squash halves in the slow cooker, cut side down. Add olive oil, garlic, and salt. Cover and cook on low for 4 hours. Scrape into strands and toss with pesto before serving.

N.V.: Cal. 180 | Fat 10g | Carb. 22g | Prot. 3g

SLOW COOKER GOLDEN CHICKPEAS WITH CUMIN & CORIANDER

P.T.: 5 minutes (preparation), 5 hours (cooking)

Ingr.:

- ½ cup canned chickpeas, drained
- 1 ½ cups vegetable broth
- ½ tsp turmeric
- ½ tsp ground cumin
- ½ tsp ground coriander

Serv.: 2

Cooking Method: Slow Cooker

Procedure:

Place chickpeas, broth, turmeric, cumin, and coriander in the slow cooker, stirring gently. Cover and cook on low for 5 hours until chickpeas absorb the flavors. Stir before serving warm.

N.V.: Cal. 200 | Fat 3g | Carb. 34g | Prot. 9g

Chapter 6: Healing Drinks & Elixirs for All-Day Energy

GOLDEN TURMERIC LATTE WITH COCONUT & CINNAMON

P.T.: 5 minutes (preparation), 3 hours (cooking)

Ingr.:

- 1 ½ cups coconut milk
- ½ tsp turmeric
- ½ tsp cinnamon
- 1 tsp honey
- ½ tsp vanilla extract

Serv.: 2

Cooking Method: Slow Cooker

Procedure:

Combine coconut milk, turmeric, cinnamon, honey, and vanilla extract in the slow cooker, stirring gently. Cover and cook on low for 3 hours, stirring occasionally. Serve warm, whisking before pouring to blend flavors.

N.V.: Cal. 190 | Fat 14g | Carb. 12g | Prot. 2g

SLOW COOKER ANTI-INFLAMMATORY GINGER & LEMON TEA

P.T.: 5 minutes (preparation), 3 hours (cooking)

Ingr.:

- 4 cups water
- 1 tbsp grated ginger
- 1 tbsp lemon juice
- 1 tsp honey
- ½ tsp turmeric

Serv.: 2

Cooking Method: Slow Cooker

Procedure:

Add water, ginger, lemon juice, honey, and turmeric to the slow cooker, stirring well. Cover and cook on low for 3 hours, allowing the flavors to infuse. Strain before serving warm or chilled.

N.V.: Cal. 30 | Fat 0g | Carb. 8g | Prot. 0g

COCONUT CHAI SPICED ELIXIR WITH CARDAMOM & CLOVES

P.T.: 5 minutes (preparation), 4 hours (cooking)

Ingr.:

- 1 ½ cups coconut milk
- ½ tsp ground cardamom
- ½ tsp ground cloves
- ½ tsp cinnamon
- 1 tsp honey

Serv.: 2

Cooking Method: Slow Cooker

Procedure:

Combine coconut milk, cardamom, cloves, cinnamon, and honey in the slow cooker, stirring gently.

Cover and cook on low for 4 hours, stirring occasionally. Serve warm, whisking before pouring.

N.V.: Cal. 200 | Fat 15g | Carb. 14g | Prot. 2g

SLOW COOKER APPLE CIDER VINEGAR DETOX TONIC

P.T.: 5 minutes (preparation), 3 hours (cooking)

Ingr.:

- 4 cups water
- 1 tbsp apple cider vinegar
- 1 small apple, sliced
- ½ tsp cinnamon
- 1 tsp honey

Serv.: 2

Cooking Method: Slow Cooker

Procedure:

Place water, apple cider vinegar, apple slices, cinnamon, and honey in the slow cooker, stirring gently. Cover and cook on low for 3 hours, allowing the flavors to blend. Strain and serve warm or chilled.

N.V.: Cal. 40 | Fat 0g | Carb. 10g | Prot. 0g

MATCHA GREEN TEA & COCONUT COLLAGEN LATTE

P.T.: 5 minutes (preparation), 2 hours (cooking)

Ingr.:

- 1 ½ cups coconut milk
- ½ tsp matcha powder
- 1 scoop collagen powder
- 1 tsp honey
- ½ tsp vanilla extract

Serv.: 2

Cooking Method: Slow Cooker

Procedure:

Whisk coconut milk, matcha, collagen, honey, and vanilla in the slow cooker. Cover and cook on low for 2 hours, stirring occasionally. Blend or whisk before serving for a creamy texture.

N.V.: Cal. 180 | Fat 12g | Carb. 10g | Prot. 6g

SLOW COOKER HIBISCUS & GINGER HYDRATION INFUSION

P.T.: 5 minutes (preparation), 3 hours (cooking)

Ingr.:

- 4 cups water
- 2 tbsp dried hibiscus petals
- 1 tbsp grated ginger
- 1 tsp honey
- ½ tsp lemon juice

Serv.: 2

Cooking Method: Slow Cooker

Procedure:

Place water, hibiscus, ginger, honey, and lemon juice in the slow cooker, stirring gently. Cover and cook on low for 3 hours, then strain and serve warm or over ice.

N.V.: Cal. 35 | Fat 0g | Carb. 9g | Prot. 0g

ANTI-INFLAMMATORY BONE BROTH WITH GARLIC & TURMERIC

P.T.: 5 minutes (preparation), 6 hours (cooking)

Ingr.:

- 4 cups bone broth
- ½ tsp turmeric
- ½ tsp minced garlic
- ½ tsp black pepper
- 1 tsp apple cider vinegar

Serv.: 2

Cooking Method: Slow Cooker

Procedure:

Combine bone broth, turmeric, garlic, black pepper, and apple cider vinegar in the slow cooker.

Cover and cook on low for 6 hours, stirring occasionally. Serve warm, whisking before pouring.

N.V.: Cal. 80 | Fat 2g | Carb. 2g | Prot. 9g

CINNAMON-SPICED ALMOND MILK WITH MACA & HONEY

P.T.: 5 minutes (preparation), 3 hours (cooking)

Ingr.:

- 1 ½ cups almond milk
- ½ tsp cinnamon
- ½ tsp maca powder
- 1 tsp honey
- ½ tsp vanilla extract

Serv.: 2

Cooking Method: Slow Cooker

Procedure:

Combine almond milk, cinnamon, maca powder, honey, and vanilla in the slow cooker, stirring gently. Cover and cook on low for 3 hours, stirring occasionally. Serve warm.

N.V.: Cal. 120 | Fat 5g | Carb. 14g | Prot. 3g

SLOW COOKER DETOXIFYING DANDELION ROOT TEA

P.T.: 5 minutes (preparation), 4 hours (cooking)

Ingr.:

- 4 cups water
- 1 tbsp dried dandelion root
- 1 tsp grated ginger
- 1 tsp lemon juice
- 1 tsp honey

Serv.: 2

Cooking Method: Slow Cooker

Procedure:

Place water, dandelion root, ginger, lemon juice, and honey in the slow cooker, stirring gently. Cover and cook on low for 4 hours, then strain and serve warm.

N.V.: Cal. 30 | Fat 0g | Carb. 8g | Prot. 0g

ANTI-INFLAMMATORY BLUEBERRY & BASIL TONIC

P.T.: 5 minutes (preparation), 3 hours (cooking)

Ingr.:

- 4 cups water
- ½ cup fresh blueberries
- 3 basil leaves, torn
- 1 tsp honey
- ½ tsp lemon juice

Serv.: 2

Cooking Method: Slow Cooker

Procedure:

Add water, blueberries, basil, honey, and lemon juice to the slow cooker, stirring gently. Cover and cook on low for 3 hours, then strain and serve warm or chilled.

N.V.: Cal. 40 | Fat 0g | Carb. 10g | Prot. 0g

SLOW COOKER CACAO & REISHI MUSHROOM HOT CHOCOLATE

P.T.: 5 minutes (preparation), 3 hours (cooking)

Ingr.:

- 1 ½ cups almond milk
- 1 tbsp cacao powder
- ½ tsp reishi mushroom powder
- 1 tsp honey
- ½ tsp vanilla extract

Serv.: 2

Cooking Method: Slow Cooker

Procedure:

Combine almond milk, cacao powder, reishi mushroom powder, honey, and vanilla extract in the slow cooker, stirring well. Cover and cook on low for 3 hours, stirring occasionally. Serve warm, whisking before pouring.

N.V.: Cal. 140 | Fat 5g | Carb. 18g | Prot. 3g

GUT-HEALING ALOE VERA & LEMON ELIXIR

P.T.: 5 minutes (preparation), 2 hours (cooking)

Ingr.:

- 4 cups water
- ½ cup fresh aloe vera juice
- 1 tbsp lemon juice
- 1 tsp honey
- ½ tsp grated ginger

Serv.: 2

Cooking Method: Slow Cooker

Procedure:

Place water, aloe vera juice, lemon juice, honey, and ginger in the slow cooker, stirring gently. Cover and cook on low for 2 hours, then strain and serve warm or chilled.

N.V.: Cal. 35 | Fat 0g | Carb. 9g | Prot. 0g

SLOW COOKER MINT & FENNEL DIGESTION TISANE

P.T.: 5 minutes (preparation), 3 hours (cooking)

Ingr.:

- 4 cups water
- 1 tbsp fennel seeds
- 5 fresh mint leaves
- ½ tsp honey
- ½ tsp lemon juice

Serv.: 2

Cooking Method: Slow Cooker

Procedure:

Add water, fennel seeds, mint leaves, honey, and lemon juice to the slow cooker, stirring well. Cover and cook on low for 3 hours, allowing the flavors to infuse. Strain before serving warm.

N.V.: Cal. 30 | Fat 0g | Carb. 7g | Prot. 0g

SPICED PUMPKIN & COCONUT HEALING SMOOTHIE

P.T.: 5 minutes (preparation), 3 hours (cooking)

Ingr.:

- 1 cup pumpkin purée
- 1 ½ cups coconut milk
- ½ tsp cinnamon
- ½ tsp turmeric
- 1 tsp honey

Serv.: 2

Cooking Method: Slow Cooker

Procedure:

Combine pumpkin purée, coconut milk, cinnamon, turmeric, and honey in the slow cooker, stirring well. Cover and cook on low for 3 hours, then blend until smooth. Serve warm or chilled.

N.V.: Cal. 180 | Fat 10g | Carb. 20g | Prot. 3g

SLOW COOKER LAVENDER & CHAMOMILE RELAXATION TEA

P.T.: 5 minutes (preparation), 3 hours (cooking)

Ingr.:

- 4 cups water
- 1 tbsp dried lavender
- 1 tbsp dried chamomile
- 1 tsp honey
- ½ tsp vanilla extract

Serv.: 2

Cooking Method: Slow Cooker

Procedure:

Place water, lavender, chamomile, honey, and vanilla extract in the slow cooker, stirring gently.

Cover and cook on low for 3 hours, then strain and serve warm.

N.V.: Cal. 30 | Fat 0g | Carb. 8g | Prot. 0g

Chapter 7: Naturally Sweet Treats Without the Guilt

SLOW COOKER GOLDEN TURMERIC & COCONUT RICE PUDDING

P.T.: 5 minutes (preparation), 4 hours (cooking)

Ingr.:

- ½ cup jasmine rice
- 1 ½ cups coconut milk
- ½ tsp turmeric
- 1 tbsp maple syrup
- ½ tsp vanilla extract

Serv.: 2

Cooking Method: Slow Cooker

Procedure:

Combine rice, coconut milk, turmeric, and maple syrup in the slow cooker, stirring gently. Cover and cook on low for 4 hours until thick and creamy. Stir in vanilla extract before serving warm.

N.V.: Cal. 230 | Fat 12g | Carb. 30g | Prot. 3g

CINNAMON-SPICED BAKED APPLES WITH WALNUTS & DATES

P.T.: 5 minutes (preparation), 3 hours (cooking)

Ingr.:

- 2 small apples, cored
- 2 tbsp chopped walnuts
- 2 tbsp chopped dates
- ½ tsp cinnamon
- 1 tsp honey

Serv.: 2

Cooking Method: Slow Cooker

Procedure:

Stuff apples with walnuts, dates, and cinnamon, then drizzle with honey. Place in the slow cooker and cover. Cook on low for 3 hours until tender, then serve warm.

N.V.: Cal. 210 | Fat 6g | Carb. 38g | Prot. 2g

SLOW COOKER ANTI-INFLAMMATORY SWEET POTATO BROWNIES

P.T.: 5 minutes (preparation), 4 hours (cooking)

Ingr.:

- ½ cup mashed sweet potato
- ¼ cup cacao powder
- 2 tbsp almond flour
- 1 tbsp maple syrup
- ½ tsp vanilla extract

Serv.: 2

Cooking Method: Slow Cooker

Procedure:

Mix all ingredients in a bowl until smooth, then transfer to the slow cooker. Cover and cook on low for 4 hours until firm. Let cool slightly before slicing and serving.

N.V.: Cal. 220 | Fat 7g | Carb. 30g | Prot. 4g

HEALING GINGER & HONEY POACHED PEARS

P.T.: 5 minutes (preparation), 3 hours (cooking)

Ingr.:

- 2 small pears, peeled
- 1 ½ cups water
- ½ tsp grated ginger
- 1 tbsp honey
- ½ tsp cinnamon

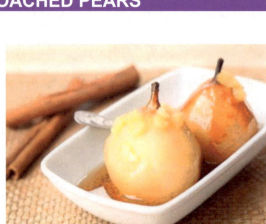

Serv.: 2

Cooking Method: Slow Cooker

Procedure:

Place pears, water, ginger, honey, and cinnamon in the slow cooker, stirring gently. Cover and cook on low for 3 hours until pears are soft. Serve warm with syrup from the slow cooker.

N.V.: Cal. 180 | Fat 1g | Carb. 40g | Prot. 1g

SLOW COOKER ALMOND BUTTER & CACAO ENERGY BITES

P.T.: 5 minutes (preparation), 2 hours (cooking)

Ingr.:

- ¼ cup almond butter
- 2 tbsp cacao powder
- ¼ cup rolled oats
- 1 tbsp honey
- ½ tsp vanilla extract

Serv.: 2

Cooking Method: Slow Cooker

Procedure:

Mix all ingredients in a bowl until well combined, then shape into small balls. Place in the slow cooker and cook on low for 2 hours. Let cool before serving.

N.V.: Cal. 210 | Fat 12g | Carb. 22g | Prot. 5g

SPICED CARROT CAKE OATMEAL BARS

P.T.: 5 minutes (preparation), 3 hours (cooking)

Ingr.:

- ½ cup rolled oats
- ¼ cup grated carrots
- 1 tbsp maple syrup
- ½ tsp cinnamon
- ½ tsp vanilla extract

Serv.: 2

Cooking Method: Slow Cooker

Procedure:

Mix oats, carrots, maple syrup, cinnamon, and vanilla in a bowl until combined. Pour into the slow cooker and cook on low for 3 hours until firm. Let cool before slicing.

N.V.: Cal. 190 | Fat 3g | Carb. 34g | Prot. 4g

SLOW COOKER CHIA & BLUEBERRY JAM WITH MAPLE SYRUP

P .T.: 5 minutes (preparation), 2 hours (cooking)

Ingr.:

- 1 cup blueberries
- 2 tbsp chia seeds
- 1 tbsp maple syrup
- ½ tsp lemon juice
- ½ cup water

Serv.: 2

Cooking Method: Slow Cooker

Procedure:

Combine all ingredients in the slow cooker, stirring gently. Cover and cook on low for 2 hours, stirring occasionally. Let cool before serving as a spread or topping.

N.V.: Cal. 110 | Fat 2g | Carb. 22g | Prot. 2g

GOLDEN CASHEW & TURMERIC FUDGE

P.T.: 5 minutes (preparation), 3 hours (cooking)

Ingr.:

- ¼ cup cashew butter
- 1 tbsp coconut oil
- ½ tsp turmeric
- 1 tbsp honey
- ½ tsp vanilla extract

Serv.: 2

Cooking Method: Slow Cooker

Procedure:

Combine all ingredients in the slow cooker, stirring well. Cover and cook on low for 3 hours, stirring occasionally. Pour into a mold, let cool, and refrigerate until firm.

N.V.: Cal. 240 | Fat 16g | Carb. 18g | Prot. 4g

SLOW COOKER DARK CHOCOLATE & AVOCADO MOUSSE

P.T.: 5 minutes (preparation), 2 hours (cooking)

Ingr.:

- 1 ripe avocado
- 2 tbsp cacao powder
- 1 tbsp honey
- ½ tsp vanilla extract
- ½ cup almond milk

Serv.: 2

Cooking Method: Slow Cooker

Procedure:

Blend all ingredients until smooth, then transfer to the slow cooker. Cover and cook on low for 2 hours, stirring occasionally. Let cool slightly before serving.

N.V.: Cal. 200 | Fat 12g | Carb. 22g | Prot. 3g

COCONUT & MATCHA SLOW COOKER MACAROONS

P.T.: 5 minutes (preparation), 3 hours (cooking)

Ingr.:

- ½ cup shredded coconut
- 1 tbsp matcha powder
- 1 tbsp honey
- ½ tsp vanilla extract
- 1 egg white

Serv.: 2

Cooking Method: Slow Cooker

Procedure:

Mix all ingredients in a bowl until combined, then shape into small mounds. Place in the slow cooker and cook on low for 3 hours until set. Let cool before serving.

N.V.: Cal. 180 | Fat 12g | Carb. 16g | Prot. 3g

SLOW COOKER GINGERBREAD-SPICED QUINOA PUDDING

P.T.: 5 minutes (preparation), 4 hours (cooking)

Ingr.:

- ½ cup quinoa, rinsed
- 1 ½ cups almond milk
- ½ tsp cinnamon
- ½ tsp ground ginger
- 1 tbsp maple syrup

Serv.: 2

Cooking Method: Slow Cooker

Procedure:

Place quinoa, almond milk, cinnamon, ginger, and maple syrup in the slow cooker, stirring gently.

Cover and cook on low for 4 hours until thick and creamy. Stir before serving warm.

N.V.: Cal. 220 | Fat 6g | Carb. 36g | Prot. 8g

HONEY-ROASTED PINEAPPLE WITH CINNAMON & MINT

P.T.: 5 minutes (preparation), 3 hours (cooking)

Ingr.:

- 1 cup pineapple chunks
- 1 tbsp honey
- ½ tsp cinnamon
- 1 tsp lime juice
- 2 fresh mint leaves, chopped

Serv.: 2

Cooking Method: Slow Cooker

Procedure:

Toss pineapple with honey, cinnamon, and lime juice, then place in the slow cooker. Cover and cook on low for 3 hours until caramelized. Stir in chopped mint before serving warm.

N.V.: Cal. 150 | Fat 0g | Carb. 38g | Prot. 1g

SLOW COOKER BLACKBERRY & BASIL COMPOTE

P.T.: 5 minutes (preparation), 2 hours (cooking)

Ingr.:

- 1 cup blackberries
- 1 tbsp honey
- ½ tsp lemon juice
- 2 fresh basil leaves, chopped
- ½ cup water

Serv.: 2

Cooking Method: Slow Cooker

Procedure:

Combine blackberries, honey, lemon juice, basil, and water in the slow cooker, stirring gently. Cover and cook on low for 2 hours until soft. Mash lightly before serving warm or chilled.

N.V.: Cal. 90 | Fat 0g | Carb. 22g | Prot. 1g

SPICED PUMPKIN & PECAN SLOW COOKER BLONDIES

P.T.: 5 minutes (preparation), 4 hours (cooking)

Ingr.:

- ½ cup pumpkin purée
- ¼ cup almond flour
- 1 tbsp maple syrup
- ½ tsp cinnamon
- 2 tbsp chopped pecans

Serv.: 2

Cooking Method: Slow Cooker

Procedure:

Mix all ingredients in a bowl until smooth, then transfer to the slow cooker. Cover and cook on low for 4 hours until firm. Let cool before slicing into squares.

N.V.: Cal. 210 | Fat 10g | Carb. 24g | Prot. 4g

SLOW COOKER DATE & WALNUT ENERGY BARS

P.T.: 5 minutes (preparation), 3 hours (cooking)

Ingr.:

- ½ cup pitted dates
- ¼ cup chopped walnuts
- 1 tbsp almond butter
- ½ tsp cinnamon
- ½ tsp vanilla extract

Serv.: 2

Cooking Method: Slow Cooker

Procedure:

Blend dates, walnuts, almond butter, cinnamon, and vanilla into a paste, then press into a lined slow cooker. Cover and cook on low for 3 hours until firm. Let cool before cutting into bars.

N.V.: Cal. 230 | Fat 12g | Carb. 30g | Prot. 5g

Chapter 8: 30-Day Meal Plan & Shopping Guide

Following an anti-inflammatory diet becomes effortless when there's a plan in place. A structured 30-day meal plan removes guesswork, ensuring every meal is balanced, nourishing, and easy to prepare. By focusing on budget-friendly ingredients and simple slow cooker recipes, this guide makes it possible to eat for health without added stress. Customizing the plan for specific goals—whether weight loss, sustained energy, or gut healing—allows for flexibility while maintaining the core principles of anti-inflammatory eating.

The 30-Day Plan

Day	Breakfast	Lunch	Dinner	Snack
Day 1	Warm Banana Walnut Breakfast Bake	Slow Cooker Cabbage & Fennel Detox Soup	Slow Cooker Zesty Lime & Cilantro Chicken Tacos	Slow Cooker Lavender & Chamomile Relaxation Tea
Day 2	Walnut & Dark Cherry Slow Cooker Granola	Tomato, Basil & Cannellini Bean Healing Stew	Slow Cooker Coconut-Curry Meatballs	Spiced Pumpkin & Coconut Healing Smoothie
Day 3	Slow Cooker Almond Butter & Flaxseed Breakfast Bars	Gut-Healing Miso & Shiitake Mushroom Broth	Ginger-Turmeric Cauliflower & Chickpea Tagine	Anti-Inflammatory Bone Broth with Garlic & Turmeric
Day 4	Golden Turmeric Oatmeal with Chia & Almonds	Slow Cooker Curried Sweet Potato & Coconut Soup	Healing Lemon, Dill & Garlic Salmon Fillets	Cinnamon-Spiced Baked Apples with Walnuts & Dates
Day 5	Golden Turmeric Oatmeal with Chia & Almonds	Healing Bone Broth & Mushroom Elixir	Anti-Inflammatory Butternut Squash & Black Bean Tacos	Slow Cooker Golden Turmeric & Coconut Rice Pudding
Day 6	Anti-Inflammatory Golden Raisin & Ginger Millet Porridge	Soothing Carrot, Turmeric & Apple Soup	Slow Cooker Lemon-Garlic Chicken with Turmeric & Rosemary	Slow Cooker Detoxifying Dandelion Root Tea

Day 7	Slow Cooker Berry & Hemp Seed Breakfast Crumble	Slow Cooker Spiced Pumpkin & Coconut Soup	Ginger-Turmeric Cauliflower & Chickpea Tagine	Slow Cooker Apple Cider Vinegar Detox Tonic
Day 8	Anti-Inflammatory Sweet Potato & Ginger Breakfast Mash	Golden Turmeric & Ginger Carrot Soup	Slow Cooker Honey-Garlic Chicken with Broccoli & Carrots	Anti-Inflammatory Bone Broth with Garlic & Turmeric
Day 9	Berry Bliss Overnight Slow Cooker Chia Pudding	Slow Cooker Spiced Pumpkin & Coconut Soup	Anti-Inflammatory Garlic & Turmeric Balsamic Beef Roast	Healing Ginger & Honey Poached Pears
Day 10	Healing Apple Cider Vinegar & Honey Oatmeal	Spiced Red Pepper & Almond Soup	Spiced Butternut Squash & Red Lentil Stew	Slow Cooker Detoxifying Dandelion Root Tea
Day 11	Cinnamon-Spiced Apple Quinoa Porridge	Detoxifying Green Soup with Kale & Broccoli	Golden Cauliflower & Lentil Curry with Coconut Milk	Matcha Green Tea & Coconut Collagen Latte
Day 12	Coconut & Almond Butter Slow Cooker Breakfast Cake	Lemon-Ginger Detox Lentil Soup	Slow Cooker Lemon-Garlic Chicken with Turmeric & Rosemary	Golden Turmeric Latte with Coconut & Cinnamon
Day 13	Warm Banana Walnut Breakfast Bake	Golden Turmeric & Ginger Carrot Soup	Healing Lemon, Dill & Garlic Salmon Fillets	Healing Ginger & Honey Poached Pears
Day 14	Slow Cooker Almond Butter & Flaxseed Breakfast Bars	Anti-Inflammatory Butternut Squash & Apple Soup	Anti-Inflammatory Ginger-Turmeric Salmon with Coconut Broth	Slow Cooker Detoxifying Dandelion Root Tea
Day 15	Slow Cooker Blueberry Basil Chia Pudding	Slow Cooker Cabbage & Fennel Detox Soup	Healing Turmeric & Ginger Beef Stew	Slow Cooker Anti-Inflammatory Sweet Potato Brownies

Day 16	Warm Banana Walnut Breakfast Bake	Slow Cooker Curried Sweet Potato & Coconut Soup	Healing Lemon, Dill & Garlic Salmon Fillets	Slow Cooker Lavender & Chamomile Relaxation Tea
Day 17	Slow Cooker Ginger-Turmeric Pear Compote	Slow Cooker Curried Sweet Potato & Coconut Soup	Slow Cooker Garlic & Herb Quinoa-Stuffed Peppers	Golden Turmeric Latte with Coconut & Cinnamon
Day 18	Pumpkin & Cinnamon Spiced Overnight Steel-Cut Oats	Slow Cooker Curried Sweet Potato & Coconut Soup	Slow Cooker Cinnamon & Ginger-Spiced Turkey Chili	Anti-Inflammatory Blueberry & Basil Tonic
Day 19	Golden Turmeric Oatmeal with Chia & Almonds	Anti-Inflammatory Thai-Inspired Coconut Lemongrass Soup	Slow Cooker Lemon-Garlic Chicken with Turmeric & Rosemary	Anti-Inflammatory Bone Broth with Garlic & Turmeric
Day 20	Berry Bliss Overnight Slow Cooker Chia Pudding	Tomato, Basil & Cannellini Bean Healing Stew	Spiced Butternut Squash & Red Lentil Stew	Spiced Pumpkin & Coconut Healing Smoothie
Day 21	Slow Cooker Ginger-Turmeric Pear Compote	Golden Turmeric & Ginger Carrot Soup	Slow Cooker Cinnamon & Ginger-Spiced Turkey Chili	Healing Ginger & Honey Poached Pears
Day 22	Berry Bliss Overnight Slow Cooker Chia Pudding	Anti-Inflammatory Turmeric & Cauliflower Soup	Anti-Inflammatory Garlic & Turmeric Balsamic Beef Roast	Coconut Chai Spiced Elixir with Cardamom & Cloves
Day 23	Slow Cooker Ginger-Turmeric Pear Compote	Gut-Healing Coconut, Ginger & Cauliflower Stew	Slow Cooker Coconut-Curry Meatballs	Anti-Inflammatory Bone Broth with Garlic & Turmeric
Day 24	Slow Cooker Matcha Coconut Rice Pudding	Spiced Red Pepper & Almond Soup	Slow Cooker Honey-Garlic Chicken with Broccoli & Carrots	Matcha Green Tea & Coconut Collagen Latte

Day 25	Warm Banana Walnut Breakfast Bake	Anti-Inflammatory Butternut Squash & Apple Soup	Slow Cooker Honey-Garlic Chicken with Broccoli & Carrots	Gut-Healing Aloe Vera & Lemon Elixir
Day 26	Slow Cooker Blueberry Basil Chia Pudding	Soothing Carrot, Turmeric & Apple Soup	Slow Cooker Coconut-Lime Shrimp with Zoodles	Coconut Chai Spiced Elixir with Cardamom & Cloves
Day 27	Slow Cooker Matcha Coconut Rice Pudding	Soothing Carrot, Turmeric & Apple Soup	Slow Cooker Zesty Lime & Cilantro Chicken Tacos	Cinnamon-Spiced Almond Milk with Maca & Honey
Day 28	Coconut Golden Milk Breakfast Farro	Slow Cooker Red Lentil & Tomato Healing Stew	Slow Cooker Moroccan-Spiced Chickpeas & Sweet Potatoes	Slow Cooker Anti-Inflammatory Sweet Potato Brownies
Day 29	Anti-Inflammatory Sweet Potato & Ginger Breakfast Mash	Slow Cooker Spiced Pumpkin & Coconut Soup	Spiced Butternut Squash & Red Lentil Stew	Slow Cooker Golden Turmeric & Coconut Rice Pudding
Day 30	Pumpkin & Cinnamon Spiced Overnight Steel-Cut Oats	Ginger-Garlic Chicken Soup for Immunity	Anti-Inflammatory Garlic & Turmeric Balsamic Beef Roast	Slow Cooker Lavender & Chamomile Relaxation Tea

Complete Shopping List for Budget-Friendly Ingredients

PANTRY STAPLES (SHELF-STABLE & DRY GOODS)

- **Grains & Seeds**
  - Rolled oats
  - Steel-cut oats
  - Quinoa
  - Brown rice
  - Millet
  - Farro

- Chia seeds
- Flaxseeds
- Hemp seeds
- **Legumes & Beans**
  - Canned or dried chickpeas
  - Canned or dried lentils (red, green)

- o Cannellini beans
  - o Black beans
- **Flours & Baking Essentials**
  - o Almond flour
  - o Coconut flour
  - o Baking powder
  - o Baking soda
- **Nuts & Nut Butters**
  - o Almonds
  - o Walnuts
  - o Cashews
  - o Pecans
  - o Almond butter
- **Sweeteners & Natural Syrups**
  - o Maple syrup
  - o Honey
  - o Medjool dates
- **Dried Fruits**
  - o Golden raisins
  - o Dried cherries
  - o Dried blueberries
  - o Dried cranberries

- **Canned & Jarred Goods**
  - o Coconut milk (full-fat & lite)
  - o Tomato paste
  - o Diced tomatoes
  - o Apple cider vinegar
- **Oils & Healthy Fats**
  - o Extra virgin olive oil
  - o Coconut oil
  - o Avocado oil
- **Herbs & Spices**
  - o Cinnamon
  - o Turmeric
  - o Ginger (ground & fresh)
  - o Cardamom
  - o Cloves
  - o Cumin
  - o Coriander
  - o Smoked paprika
  - o Black pepper
  - o Nutmeg
  - o Sea salt

FRESH PRODUCE (BUDGET-FRIENDLY & NUTRIENT-DENSE)

- Apples
- Bananas
- Pears
- Berries (blueberries, strawberries)
- Oranges
- Lemons
- Limes
- Sweet potatoes
- Carrots
- Beets

- Butternut squash
- Cauliflower
- Broccoli
- Brussels sprouts
- Kale
- Spinach
- Zucchini
- Bell peppers
- Garlic
- Onions

- Ginger root
- Fresh basil
- Fresh mint
- Fresh cilantro

PROTEINS & DAIRY ALTERNATIVES

- Bone broth
- Organic or pasture-raised eggs
- Salmon fillets (fresh or frozen)
- Chicken breasts (fresh or frozen)
- Grass-fed beef (stew meat, ground beef)
- Turkey (ground turkey or turkey breast)
- Shrimp (frozen, wild-caught)
- Tofu (firm or extra firm)
- Unsweetened almond milk
- Unsweetened coconut yogurt

How to Customize the Meal Plan for Weight Loss, Energy, or Gut Healing

A meal plan is only as effective as it is personal. No two bodies are the same, and while a structured anti-inflammatory plan lays the groundwork for better health, individual goals shape how it's applied. Whether the focus is weight loss, sustained energy, or gut healing, small adjustments fine-tune the plan to work for specific needs without sacrificing convenience or flavor.

For weight loss, the priority is **balancing satiety with calorie efficiency.** Slow-cooked meals naturally lend themselves to this approach, as they maximize fiber and protein while keeping unnecessary additives out of the equation. The most effective shift is adjusting portion sizes of higher-calorie ingredients while maintaining the volume of nutrient-dense foods. Hearty legumes, leafy greens, and cruciferous vegetables provide bulk without excess calories, keeping meals satisfying. Protein selection also plays a role—leaner cuts of poultry, wild-caught fish, and plant-based proteins like lentils offer muscle support without unnecessary fats. Healthy fats remain crucial, but portioning matters. Instead of pouring oil freely, measuring amounts ensures the right balance between nourishment and calorie control. Slow-cooked soups and stews work particularly well, as they allow for generous portions without overloading on high-calorie components.

For sustained energy, the key is **stabilizing blood sugar while supporting metabolic endurance.** This means prioritizing complex carbohydrates that digest slowly, providing a steady fuel source rather than a quick spike and crash. Root vegetables like sweet potatoes, beets, and carrots deliver long-lasting energy while supplying critical micronutrients. Pairing them with high-quality proteins— whether pastured eggs, grass-fed beef, or plant-based sources like hemp seeds—helps regulate insulin response and prevent mid-day fatigue. Meal timing also influences energy levels. Eating balanced meals at consistent intervals maintains metabolic efficiency, preventing energy dips caused by erratic fueling. Incorporating slow-cooked breakfasts, such as protein-rich oatmeals or spiced chia puddings, starts the day with sustained nourishment rather than a temporary caffeine-fueled boost.

For gut healing, the focus shifts to **reducing inflammation, supporting digestion, and strengthening the microbiome.** Meals should be easy on the digestive system, which means prioritizing **cooked foods over raw,** as slow cooking naturally breaks down fibers that can sometimes cause irritation. Bone broth becomes a cornerstone, delivering collagen and amino acids that repair the gut lining and enhance nutrient absorption. Fermented ingredients, like miso or coconut yogurt, introduce beneficial probiotics that balance gut bacteria, while prebiotic-rich foods—onions, garlic, and asparagus—feed that healthy flora. Spices play an essential role as well. Turmeric and ginger actively reduce gut inflammation, while cinnamon helps regulate digestive enzymes. Consistency is what makes gut healing effective. Sticking with gentle, nourishing meals and avoiding inflammatory triggers ensures the digestive system can rebuild its strength over time.

Adjusting a meal plan to fit specific health goals isn't about making drastic changes—it's about **small, strategic tweaks** that enhance results while maintaining the simplicity that makes slow-cooked, anti-inflammatory meals sustainable. The right adjustments turn a standard plan into a deeply personalized approach, ensuring long-term success without complication.

Conclusion: Your Path to a Healthier, Pain-Free Life

Healing starts with food, but lasting change comes from making the right choices easy and sustainable. Anti-inflammatory eating isn't about following rigid rules or chasing perfection—it's about creating habits that naturally support the body. When stress is removed from the equation and food becomes a tool for nourishment rather than restriction, eating well stops feeling like an effort and becomes second nature.

How to Keep Up with Anti-Inflammatory Eating Without Stress

Sticking with an anti-inflammatory way of eating isn't about perfection. The biggest mistake people make is thinking they have to follow every rule without fail, that one misstep erases all progress. That kind of rigid mindset creates stress, and stress itself is one of the most inflammatory things you can put your body through. The real key to making this work long-term isn't in strict discipline—it's in making it so effortless that it becomes second nature.

Food should never feel like a burden. The easiest way to eliminate stress around anti-inflammatory eating is to remove decision fatigue. Having a handful of go-to meals that come together without much thought makes all the difference. When your kitchen is stocked with ingredients that align with your health goals, the hard part is already done. There's no need to constantly plan elaborate meals. A slow cooker filled with simple, whole ingredients will always yield something nourishing, whether it's a comforting soup, a slow-simmered stew, or a batch of flavorful roasted vegetables.

Routines make consistency possible without requiring willpower. When healthy meals are already prepared, there's no scramble to figure out what to eat after a long day. Meal prepping doesn't have to mean spending an entire weekend in the kitchen. Even small steps—like chopping vegetables in advance, cooking a double batch of protein, or portioning out meals for later in the week—make daily choices easier. The less effort it takes to eat well, the more likely it is to happen without stress.

Eating anti-inflammatory doesn't mean cutting out every indulgence. The goal isn't to live in deprivation, but to build a foundation where the majority of your meals support your body's healing process. If something outside of that happens occasionally, it's not a failure. The body is resilient. One meal, one day, or even one week off track doesn't erase all progress. What matters most is what happens the majority of the time. If a single choice leads to stress and guilt, that's more damaging than the food itself. Let it go and move forward.

Overcomplicating things is what makes healthy eating feel like an impossible task. Cooking doesn't need to be complex to be effective. The most powerful anti-inflammatory meals are often the simplest—slow-cooked vegetables infused with warming spices, a nourishing broth-based soup, a hearty dish built on wholesome proteins and healthy fats. The more complicated a diet feels, the harder it is to maintain. Keeping things easy means removing unnecessary obstacles.

Life will always have unpredictable moments, and waiting for the "perfect" time to commit to a way of eating will never work. The easiest way to reduce stress around food is to stop looking at it as a rigid plan and start seeing it as a flexible system. Once anti-inflammatory eating stops feeling like an effort and becomes just the way things are, stress disappears, and the body reaps the benefits without the pressure.

Making This a Long-Term Lifestyle, Not a Short-Term Diet

Lasting change doesn't come from following a set of rules for a few weeks and then going back to old habits. Diets are temporary. They're built around restriction, around the idea that food is something to be controlled rather than enjoyed. That mindset creates cycles of effort and burnout, where healthy eating feels like something you have to force yourself to do instead of something that fits seamlessly into daily life. The goal isn't to eat anti-inflammatory for a month and then move on—it's to rewire the way food is approached so that healing choices become second nature.

For a way of eating to stick long-term, it has to be flexible. Life isn't predictable, and no one eats perfectly all the time. The people who succeed in maintaining a healthy lifestyle aren't the ones who follow every guideline to the letter—they're the ones who learn how to adapt without abandoning their core habits. The best approach isn't about following strict meal plans forever. It's about understanding how to build meals that support the body, no matter the situation. Once that knowledge is in place, choices become easier, and there's no need for rigid structure.

Food should never feel like a constant decision. When something becomes routine, it stops feeling like work. The reason so many diets fail is that they require an ongoing level of effort that isn't sustainable. The easiest way to make anti-inflammatory eating last is to remove as much friction as possible. That means keeping a kitchen stocked with ingredients that make healthy meals effortless, finding go-to recipes that are simple but satisfying, and building a system where nutritious meals don't take more time or effort than less healthy alternatives. The more automatic it becomes, the less willpower it requires.

A long-term lifestyle shift happens when food is seen as nourishment, not as a set of restrictions. If a way of eating is built on deprivation, it won't last. There has to be room for enjoyment. The meals that heal the body should also be meals that are genuinely satisfying. If something feels like a sacrifice, it's only a matter of time before old habits return. When anti-inflammatory meals are built around rich flavors, satisfying textures, and deeply nourishing ingredients, there's no feeling of missing out. That's what makes it effortless to maintain.

The true power of an anti-inflammatory lifestyle lies in its simplicity. When meals are built around whole, healing ingredients and routines make healthy choices automatic, there's no need for constant discipline. Small, consistent actions lead to long-term transformation. The goal isn't temporary change but a way of eating that fits effortlessly into everyday life, bringing lasting health and energy.

Made in United States
Troutdale, OR
06/21/2025

32280592R00044